Strengthening Connections Between Education and Performance

Stanley M. Grabowski, *Editor*

NEW DIRECTIONS FOR CONTINUING EDUCATION
ALAN B. KNOX, GORDON DARKENWALD, *Editors-in-Chief*

Number 18, June 1983

Paperback sourcebooks in
The Jossey-Bass Higher Education Series

Jossey-Bass Inc., Publishers
San Francisco • Washington • London

LC
5219
.S87

Stanley M. Grabowski (Ed.).
Strengthening Connections Between Education and Performance
New Directions for Continuing Education, no. 18.
San Francisco: Jossey-Bass, 1983.

New Directions for Continuing Education Series
Alan B. Knox, Gordon Darkenwald, *Editors-in-Chief*

Copyright © 1983 by Jossey-Bass Inc., Publishers
                and
           Jossey-Bass Limited

Copyright under International, Pan American, and Universal
Copyright Conventions. All rights reserved. No part of
this issue may be reproduced in any form — except for brief
quotation (not to exceed 500 words) in a review or professional
work — without permission in writing from the publishers.

New Directions for Continuing Education (publication number
USPS 493-930) quarterly by Jossey-Bass Inc., Publishers.
Second-class postage rates paid at San Francisco, California,
and at additional mailing offices.

Correspondence:
Subscriptions, single-issue orders, change of address notices,
undelivered copies, and other correspondence should be sent to
New Directions Subscriptions, Jossey-Bass Inc., Publishers,
433 California Street, San Francisco, California 94104.

Editorial correspondence should be sent to the Editor-in-Chief,
Alan B. Knox, Teacher Education Building, Room 264,
University of Wisconsin, 225 North Mills Street, Madison,
Wisconsin 53706.

Library of Congress Catalogue Card Number LC 82-84182
International Standard Serial Number ISSN 0271-2242
International Standard Book Number ISBN 87589-944-7

Cover art by Willi Baum
Manufactured in the United States of America

Ordering Information

The paperback sourcebooks listed below are published quarterly and can be ordered either by subscription or single-copy.

Subscriptions cost $35.00 per year for institutions, agencies, and libraries. Individuals can subscribe at the special rate of $21.00 per year *if payment is by personal check.* (Note that the full rate of $35.00 applies if payment is by institutional check, even if the subscription is designated for an individual.) Standing orders are accepted. Subscriptions normally begin with the first of the four sourcebooks in the current publication year of the series. When ordering, please indicate if you prefer your subscription to begin with the first issue of the *coming* year.

Single copies are available at $7.95 when payment accompanies order, and *all single-copy orders under $25.00 must include payment.* (California, New Jersey, New York, and Washington, D.C., residents please include appropriate sales tax.) For billed orders, cost per copy is $7.95 plus postage and handling. (Prices subject to change without notice.)

Bulk orders (ten or more copies) of any individual sourcebook are available at the following discounted prices: 10-49 copies, $7.15 each; 50-100 copies, $6.35 each; over 100 copies, *inquire.* Sales tax and postage and handling charges apply as for single copy orders.

To ensure correct and prompt delivery, all orders must give either the *name of an individual* or an *official purchase order number.* Please submit your order as follows:

Subscriptions: specify series and year subscription is to begin.
Single Copies: specify sourcebook code (such as, CE8) and first two words of title.

Mail orders for United States and Possessions, Latin America, Canada, Japan, Australia, and New Zealand to:
Jossey-Bass Inc., Publishers
433 California Street
San Francisco, California 94104

Mail orders for all other parts of the world to:
Jossey-Bass Limited
28 Banner Street
London EC1Y 8QE

New Directions for Continuing Education Series
Alan B. Knox, Gordon Darkenwald, *Editors-in-Chief*

CE1 *Enhancing Proficiencies of Continuing Educators,* Alan B. Knox
CE2 *Programming for Adults Facing Mid-Life Change,* Alan B. Knox
CE3 *Assessing the Impact of Continuing Education,* Alan B. Knox
CE4 *Attracting Able Instructors of Adults,* M. Alan Brown, Harlan G. Copeland
CE5 *Providing Continuing Education by Media and Technology,* Martin N. Chamberlain

CE6 *Teaching Adults Effectively,* Alan B. Knox
CE7 *Assessing Educational Needs of Adults,* Floyd C. Pennington
CE8 *Reaching Hard-to-Reach Adults,* Gordon G. Darkenwald, Gordon A. Larson
CE9 *Strengthening Internal Support for Continuing Education,* James C. Votruba
CE10 *Advising and Counseling Adult Learners,* Frank R. DiSilvestro
CE11 *Continuing Education for Community Leadership,* Harold W. Stubblefield
CE12 *Attracting External Funds for Continuing Education,* John Buskey
CE13 *Leadership Strategies for Meeting New Challenges,* Alan B. Knox
CE14 *Programs for Older Adults,* Morris A. Okun
CE15 *Linking Philosophy and Practice,* Sharan B. Merriam
CE16 *Creative Financing and Budgeting,* Travis Shipp
CE17 *Materials for Teaching Adults: Selection, Development, and Use,* John P. Wilson

Contents

Editor's Notes 1
Stanley M. Grabowski

Chapter 1. How Educators and Trainers Can Ensure 5
On-the-Job Performance
Stanley M. Grabowski

The author suggests practical techniques that have worked in improving performance after training.

Chapter 2. Merging Instructional Technology 11
with Management Practices
Susan N. Chellino, Richard J. Walker

This chapter presents a case study method used to develop and maintain good working habits.

Chapter 3. Change Strategies Used by a Proprietary School: 21
The Dale Carnegie Organization
Paul J. Mackey

The Dale Carnegie organization uses accreditation, certificates, and pedagogic approaches to attain desired results.

Chapter 4. Effective Occupational Programs at Technical and 31
Community Colleges
James J. Corbett

Community colleges and technical institutes offer occupational technical training through hands-on experiences.

Chapter 5. Military Education and Training 37
Gordon Larson

The military uses readiness tests and other evaluations to measure the effectiveness of training.

Chapter 6. Evaluation as a Guarantee of Performance in 45
Cooperative Extension
Robert Lee Bruce

The Cooperative Extension Service uses program evaluation to increase the impact of continuing education on performance.

Chapter 7. Strengthening the Relations Between Professional Education and Performance 59
Joseph S. Gonnella, Carter Zeleznik
The medical model of continuing professional education is based on the scientific problem solving method.

Chapter 8. A Perspective on Preparing Adult Educators 73
G. L. Carter
A conceptual base for providing more adequate preparation for adult educators is presented.

Index 83

Editor's Notes

Behavioral change is one of the goals of training and education. Change may involve knowledge, skills, or attitudes and eventually will manifest itself in some kind of performance. Training and education are quite efficient for imparting knowledge and skills and, to a lesser extent, for inculcating attitudes. The main challenge to trainers and educators is to have learners transfer their newly acquired competencies into role performance.

Research and experience seem to show that there is still no single way to ensure that mastery of new learning will be transferred to actual performance. The kinds of approaches continuing educators use to increase the impact of education and training on performance will depend on numerous factors: type of sponsoring institution, organization, or agency; capacities and motives of learners; the environment; available resources, including personnel and money; and the nature of the individual's occupation or role.

The contributors to this sourcebook have reported on ways in which institutions and organizations have attempted to ensure improved performance by learners after the continuing education experience. In the first chapter, Grabowski outlines a number of suggestions offered by trainers to influence subsequent performance. Many of these techniques and tactics depend on the trainers' effectiveness as motivators. Getting learners to use their newly acquired competencies may be mostly a question of reminding them to do so, of instilling confidence, and of providing continuity through appropriate field contacts.

Chellino and Walker, in Chapter Two, look upon instructional specialists as managers with a dual responsibility—to impart skills and knowledge to workers and to satisfy organizational needs. This philosophy calls for staff and line management to collaborate with trainers in resolving organizational performance problems. Inasmuch as it must change job behavior quickly, training ought to keep to essentials, giving up elegance for efficiency and effectiveness and forming part of a performance-improvement system. Practice opportunities are one way of leading from training to implementation of new skills. The aims of training also ought to include learners' developing and maintaining good work habits. To accomplish this aim, a company needs both a policy on the use of feedback and supervisors trained in setting work standards and evaluating performance. Managers' participation is integral to the implementation and follow-up of training. Furthermore, behavior needs to be corrected, not punished.

In Chapter Three, on proprietary schools, Mackey shows how organizational accreditation is the first step toward enhancing the results of training.

Decisions about individual courses and workshops play an important role in guarantees of quick learning. Paying attention to individual learning differences also goes a long way toward rapid acquisition of competencies.

Chapter Four, on two-year educational institutions, attributes the success of occupational programs to personalized instruction. Corbett describes how courses are supplemented by other activities to meet special interests of students. For example, to make learning more realistic, technical and community colleges use extensive local trade and professional contacts. Varied formats, all based on behavioral objectives, are employed to prepare students for the world of work. Employment during school years, as well as practical, hands-on experience, are at the heart of the two-year institution's curriculum. Standards of job performance are also the standards of the classroom, and the training of individual workers becomes a total process.

In Chapter Five, on education and military training, Larson points out that training is systematically developed around objectives dictated by missions or traditions of a particular branch of the armed forces. Personnel in each occupational speciality follow prescribed sets of established training requirements, which are published in manuals for each specialty. Commanders use these manuals not only to plan training but also to evaluate training and learner proficiency. First-line supervisors use record books to keep track of each learner's ability to perform required tasks. In addition, skills-qualification tests are administered on an annual basis to ensure achievement and maintenance of skills. Systematic instructional design guarantees uniformity of acquired skills.

Chapter Six, by Bruce, focuses on evaluation as a means of ensuring high levels of performance in cooperative extension programs. Involvement in cooperative extension is mostly on the local level, where agents live among their clients. The clients evaluate and give feedback to the agents. In addition, clients are in a position to provide or withhold agents' resources, salaries, or even job security. As a quality-control tool, evaluation must be kept practical.

In Chapter Seven, Zeleznik and Gonnella discuss ways to strengthen the relationship between professional education and professional performance. They suggest that the scientific problem-solving method, with a regard for individual and group needs and values, is the one most suitable for the professions. Inadequate proficiency may result from inadequate knowledge, skills, or attitudes, which may require educational intervention to bring a substandard professional to the level of adequate performance. Administrative considerations, environmental situations, personal and medical problems, and workloads may also have adverse effects on job performance, but these factors generally do not have immediate educational implications.

One must look for correspondence between professional criteria and individual performance. In fact, the very nature of professionalization forces continuing educators to pay close attention to individuals. Thus, correcting deficiencies in performance entails determining which causes are amenable to educational intervention and then choosing an approach appropriate for a particular person.

Carter's chapter, which deals with preparing professional adult educators, provides a conceptual base for making such preparation more adequate. Carter suggests that we determine the nature of the job to be done by the professional and that we connect the theoretical aspects of adult education with professional practice. Once we have made this connection, the educational content—and the activities by which learners will encounter that content—must be fit into a learning system.

In this sourcebook, most of the examples that analyze the effect of continuing education on role performance are occupational. This is understandable, because in most work settings there are other people (supervisors and peers) besides adult learners who have a stake in improved performance, evidence of performance that provides feedback, and resources that encourage improved performance. Nevertheless, there are important types of nonoccupational continuing education programs in which application and improved performance are also important. Examples include adult basic education, family-life education, leisure education, and patient education. Still, application of skills learned in such programs may require special cooperation and effort of learners because of the absence of supervisors in nonoccupational settings. Many of the influences on transfer and application of skills discussed in this sourcebook are reflected in the following list of illustrative guidelines for increasing continuing education programs' impact on learners in these other life roles.

- Individualize learning activities to build on the learner's existing motives, abilities, and roles
- Use major standards of desired role performance as a basis of educational objectives
- Provide learners with continuing opportunities for practice and feedback, thereby enabling them to improve performance beyond specific educational activities
- Encourage learners to apply what they learn (and thus improve performance) by building their confidence in their own abilities, noting benefits of their performance, reminding them to apply what they have learned, and providing social and emotional support
- Arrange sufficient local contact among participants and providers so that individualization, standards, practice, feedback, and encouragement are likely
- Include opportunities to develop and practice strategies that alternate between new ideas (theory, knowledge, and skills) and action tasks (actual performance) in the educational program.

These methods are some of the most common ways in which continuing educators try to connect education and training with performance. There are numerous approaches used with some success by various institutions and agencies, but much more work remains to be done, both by researchers and by practitioners. Continuing education, pragmatic as it is, will always rely on "what works" as one measure of evaluation. Thus, continuing educators ought to experiment boldly in this area. Using methods reported here and elsewhere, we should also take at least some measure of risk by trying out our own ideas and hunches. If enough of us experiment for enough time and pool our findings, we may yet develop more definitive ways of strengthening connections between education and performance.

Stanley M. Grabowski
Editor

Stanley M. Grabowski is professor of education and program coordinator for continuing education at the School of Education of Boston University. He is former director of the ERIC Clearinghouse on Adult Education at Syracuse University. He recently coauthored Preparing Educators of Adults *(Jossey-Bass, 1981).*

Experience-tested techniques, used in conjunction with motivation, can produce effective and efficient job performance.

How Educators and Trainers Can Ensure On-the-Job Performance

Stanley M. Grabowski

A revolution is under way in education. It has been going on quietly and steadily at all levels for almost a generation. It is rapidly but undramatically culminating in greater demand for performance and accountability. This demand, already noticeable for some time in the private sector, has recently appeared in educational institutions because of declining enrollments. Peter F. Drucker (1981), one of the best-known management theorists, claims that the concern and demand for performance and accountability will be part of all educational endeavors, and especially of continuing education, throughout the 1980s and the 1990s.

Nevertheless, these concerns are not new to educators, who have been wrestling with them for a long time. Discussion and debate about education during the past several decades have focused in part on the tension between learning for the sake of learning and learning as an agent of change. This tension is one aspect of the broader issue of education's goals, methods, purposes, and functions. Ultimately, this issue is rooted in the philosophy and theory of learning and education.

Indeed, learning for the sake of learning has its place in education:

Houle (1961) found (and others have verified) that adults do engage in learning for its own sake. Most adults, however, pursue learning as a means to an end; for adults, learning is often associated with work, careers, and professions.

The job market requires an individual's preparation for work to contain a firm grounding in relevant competencies. This requirement becomes particularly apparent when an individual goes to a job interview. The interviewer inevitably asks the applicant, "What have you done? What kinds of experiences have you had that are relevant to the position you are applying for?" If the response to these questions is unsatisfactory, the interviewer may follow up with a question regarding capabilities, saying something like "What can you do?" Almost never does the interviewer ask simply, "What do you know?" As a result, educators have agonized over means to ensure, to some extent, that the people they teach will be able to perform on the job. This concern is especially apparent in professional and graduate schools, whose aim is to turn out professional practitioners. To be sure, professional development includes far more than acquiring basic skills and competencies, but these are the facets of a professional's life most noticeable by consumers and clients. Despite all the tests and evaluations educators perform to measure the learning of their students, there still remain concerns and questions about the impact that education has on an individual's job performance.

While trainers may make no pretense of "educating," they do share some of the concerns of educators, in light of "mounting evidence that shows that very often the training makes little or no difference in job behavior" (Mosel, 1957, p. 56). Some trainers hold an even more pessimistic view of training; Lusterman (1977) quotes a steel-industry executive as saying, "Training has often been a form of entertainment in industry. We have to start justifying it in terms of measured results" (p. 6). Indeed, Lusterman goes on, "many company programs have been plagued by fads, by the inappropriate application of newer techniques—courses that are taught with little concern for how, or even when, they can be applied" (p. 7).

Training prepares an individual to acquire a skill that will result in a specific kind of behavior, whereas education generally provides opportunities to live and perform better in every dimension of life. Thus, training narrows, whereas education broadens, an individual's range of responses. Both training and education, however, must prepare individuals to transfer knowledge, skills, and attitudes as conditions and circumstances change. Training, no less than education, seeks (at least implicitly) to effect change in individuals, groups, organizations, and institutions, as well as in society at large. Thus, both training and education share a proactive process of planned change (Grassi-Stimson, 1982).

Even granting that individuals are properly trained (an assumption that is open to question), there is still no assurance that learners will intuitively transfer what they have learned in the classroom to new situations on the job. If "thinking and intellectual skills tend to be tied to particular areas of knowledge, especially those exhibiting characteristics of the original teaching environment" (Stritter and Flair, 1980, p. 55), then teachers and trainers must arrange learning experiences that will facilitate the transfer of learning, as well as its application to new situations.

Learners need to know how to apply principles or examples used during training to new problems arising on the job. Most of us can appreciate this need from our experiences with mathematics courses whose teachers used simple, easy examples in the classroom, but for homework assigned difficult problems, mostly exceptions to the rules. In completing our homework assignments, we suffered immensely, because we had not grasped the principles sufficiently to be able to transfer them to more complicated and different problems.

On-the-Job Follow Through

Most teachers and trainers are skilled at imparting knowledge, but there is no guarantee that, in the absence of specific measures, the knowledge will be transferred to job performance. Once a student or a trainee leaves the learning environment, numerous factors militate against transfer and application of what has been learned. Habits are among the strongest blocks to the integration of new learning. The line of least resistance is to go back to old, comfortable ways of doing things, ways that require almost no conscious thought, because they are so much a part of us. Time is another factor of behavioral change: It simply takes a long time for an individual to integrate new learning. Many learning programs are so filled with topics that there is hardly enough time to cover them all, and even less time for the gestation process so crucial both to learning and to appropriating learning.

Even in the absence of such inhibiting factors, individuals need strong motives and incentives to use new knowledge and skills on the job. Some motives are built into some situations; for example, an individual promoted to a new position, or one who is making a career change, will tend to be highly motivated to implement newly acquired proficiencies. Not all situations have these kinds of built-in incentives, however. Situations without built-in incentives call for extraordinary approaches, which are partly in the hands of teachers and trainers and partly beyond their direct intervention. Spitzer (1982) suggests the following techniques that teachers, and particularly trainers, can use to ensure that learners will use their new proficiencies.

1. *Personal action plans.* During training, individuals prepare action plans for applying new knowledge and skills to their jobs.

2. *Group action planning.* Several individuals who work together on the job prepare a group action plan similar in format to personal action plans. The group commitment to the plan adds a dimension of mutual support when the group returns to the workplace.

3. *Multiphase programming.* The training program is divided into several parts, and trainees go back to the workplace and apply each part to their jobs before going on to the next part of training. This procedure allows trainees to apply manageable amounts of new knowledge and skills and then return to the learning environment to process their experiences.

4. *The buddy system.* By training in pairs, individuals can continue their learning interactions while providing support for each other.

5. *Performance aids.* Devices such as models, diagrams, flowcharts, checklists, tables, and decision trees can help trainees apply new learning independently. Such aids are especially crucial to the first phase of on-the-job application of new skills.

6. *Recognition systems.* Certificates, letters of merit, and similar recognition incentives can be powerful learning reinforcers.

7. *Training trainees as trainers.* When one person has to teach or train another, there is plenty of motivation for learning to apply new knowledge and skills.

8. *Contracting.* Trainees voluntarily sign contracts to implement their new proficiencies.

9. *Ample access to resources.* Providing easily accessible follow-up resources, such as trainer visits and hotline phone numbers, will provide both clarification and a demonstration of the trainer's extended commitment.

10. *Follow-up questionnaires.* Evaluation questionnaires sent to trainees shortly after training is completed will prod trainees to apply their new information and skills, give feedback on how trainees perceived the training and its practicality, and show trainees that the trainer still cares about them. Follow-up material sent to trainees for a short but regular period of time after training will encourage them to use what they have learned.

11. *Follow-up contacts.* Telephone calls and personal visits are a personal way to follow up on training and give a boost to application of new learning.

12. *Follow-up sessions.* Regular sessions, scheduled periodically after training is completed, give trainees a chance to ask questions and solve problems as they apply training to job performance. These sessions can also serve as additional evaluations of training.

Future-Oriented Performance

At their best, teaching and training are future-oriented, which is why they must be keyed to anticipated changes. First, however, teachers and trainers must help learners "put it all together." Stritter and Flair (1980) suggest an approach that includes the following elements:

1. Have learners apply and compare approaches to a given problem.
2. Have learners master the initial learning task.
3. Have the instructor discuss similar problems and compare applications of the previously used approaches.
4. Have the instructor give concrete examples and practical applications throughout the training to let learners decide which new or old approaches are most appropriate.
5. Have learners use several senses in mastering material.
6. Have learners apply their newly acquired proficiencies under conditions punctuated by irrelevant as well as disheartening elements.
7. Ask learners analytical questions in a logical, sequential order.
8. Use simulations and apprenticeships.

Despite their best efforts, there is no way trainers can present every conceivable situation that future practitioners will have to face after training. New knowledge, new procedures, and new technology will make new demands on practitioners. Thus, teaching problem-solving procedures would seem to be one way of ensuring that training will be applied on the job.

Mosel (1957) reminds us that there are three conditions required for transferring newly acquired knowledge and proficiencies to the job situation:

1. The training content must be (and must be perceived by the trainee as) useful and relevant to the job.
2. Trainees must acquire the knowledge and master the skills that constitute the training content.
3. Trainees must be sufficiently motivated to change their behavior by applying their new proficiencies to their work situations.

In summary, education and training have several components, including training to perform the immediate job, training to help the individual anticipate and accommodate changes, and training to help the individual prepare for future advancement and promotion. These kinds of training will produce workers who are not only competent to perform their immediate tasks but also, and more important, motivated to keep on learning. Clearly, there is no single way of ensuring excellent role performance. The following chapters illustrate some of the many ways institutions, associations, and organizations have attempted to improve performance.

References

Drucker, P. F. "The Coming Challenge in Our School System." *The Wall Street Journal,* March 3, 1981, p. 30.

Grassi-Stimson, L. "On Evaluating and Restructuring Training." Unpublished paper, School of Education, Boston University, 1982.

Houle, C. O. *The Inquiring Mind.* Madison: The University of Wisconsin Press, 1961.

Lusterman, S. *Education in Industry.* New York: The Conference Board, Inc., 1977.

Mosel, J. N. "Why Training Programs Fail to Carry Over." *Personnel,* 1957, *34* (3), 56–64.

Spitzer, D. R. "But Will They Use Training on the Job?" *Training/HRD,* 1982, *19* (9), pp. 48, 105.

Stritter, F. T., and Flair, M. D. *Effective Clinical Teaching.* Bethesda, Md.: National Medical Audiovisual Center/National Library of Medicine, 1980.

Stanley M. Grabowski is professor of education and program coordinator for continuing education at the School of Education of Boston University. He is former director of the ERIC Clearinghouse on Adult Education at Syracuse University. He recently coauthored Preparing Educators of Adults *(Jossey-Bass, 1981).*

To ensure improved performance and achieve organizational results, practitioners in industry must extend their efforts beyond the classroom to the workplace.

Merging Instructional Technology with Management Practices

*Susan N. Chellino
Richard J. Walker*

Instructional specialists in industry operate from two bases—commitment to educational excellence and dedication to sound business practices. Educators in this environment are usually also managers. In their training role, they are responsible for addressing the skill and knowledge requirements of employees. In their second role, they must consider the overall needs of the organization, including needs related to economic, administrative, and policy issues. Their dual role as trainer-managers permits them not only to provide effective training, when necessary, but also to fulfill a broader charge—namely, solving organizational performance problems.

An organizational problem is defined as the difference between desired and actual results (Mager and Pipe, 1970; Gilbert, 1967; Harless, 1970). Desired results are stated as objectives, work standards, or criteria for performance and are established for such work aspects as quality, quantity, efficiency, timeliness, cost-effectiveness, and accuracy. Desired results may pertain to any job, regardless of an employee's hierarchical placement or responsibilities. Actual results are obtained from measurements of work done.

The mission of trainer-managers is to rid the organization of factors causing results that are less than satisfactory. Causes may be classified broadly into three types of deficiencies—lack of proficiency, ineffective policies or methods, and unsatisfactory administration (Gilbert, 1967; Harless, 1970). The model for working on these problems is this: Deficiencies cause problems; solutions should reduce or eliminate deficiencies. In turn, these solutions will reduce or eliminate the problem.

Although trained in continuing adult education and instructional design, training specialists confront problems that may have many causes apart from lack of skill or knowledge. Thus, solutions frequently use training as one part of a multiphased remedy, but also may not include training at all.

Great care must be taken in matching solutions with problems. Solutions must satisfy the following criteria:

- Relevance—the material is needed and used on the job (Smith and Corbett, 1976)
- Transfer—information is used with equal or better proficiency on the job (Smith and Corbett, 1976)
- Design fidelity—programs, materials, and procedures must be implemented as planned
- Cost-effectiveness—solution costs less than the problem (Gilbert, 1967).

Good business practice suggests that cost-effectiveness must predominate, whatever else is done. This requirement has several implications.

First, when training is appropriate for a behavior-based deficiency (we shall not discuss the affective domain), it is directed toward the higher-order cognitive skills (described by Bloom, 1956) or toward psychomotor skills, depending on the deficient behavior. Instruction must change job behavior quickly. Consequently, those who write training programs are doing so at the level of application; little if any class time can be spent on delivering facts that will not be used. Training also must include a sufficient number of practice opportunities. A third of the instruction time should be devoted to practice (Chellino, Rice, and Dinneen, 1978). Ample practice serves several functions. It provides a frame of reference for tasks to be performed on the job, a chance to fail in a controlled environment without the normal consequences, and the ability to apply new skills self-sufficiently and almost immediately.

Second, the question of a problem's duration is a crucial one and must be examined from two perspectives. To field managers experiencing a problem, the length of time it remains unsolved is translated into costs for which there is no productive return. Trainers alert to this situation must respond quickly, and this response is made in several ways. Information that is not readily convertible to action ought to be minimized and, when possible, eliminated. Trainers are urged to delete "nice to know" information in favor of "need to know" information. Harless (1970) says that delivering too much "why" about a subject obscures the "how." The emphasis should be on behavioral change.

Third, training must be effective and efficient, without necessarily being elegant. For example, a modest delivery medium may be used instead of elaborate audiovisual displays. If the end product is improved on-the-job performance, then the means for enabling it need not be spectacular. Plain materials, easily understood and applied, should predominate over sophisticated designs.

Fourth, training is often only part of a more encompassing performance-improvement system. Plans may include such nontraining elements as changes in work methods, policy, equipment, or forms of administration. Components of a multiphased program must be adapted to a format that will produce the needed improvement.

Finally, the design and development of solutions must be accompanied by their successful implementation. No matter how good a solution is, the problem will continue unless local management accepts the solution the way it was designed. Employees must be allowed to apply their new knowledge and, with their supervisors' support, use new methods on the job. When training is the solution, support means letting employees do what they have been trained do to in the way they were trained to do it. When training has been prescribed along with combinations of other solutions, support means removing obstacles and encouraging, even rewarding, use of the new methods. Support is most likely to be forthcoming when supervisors are convinced that the solutions fit the problems.

Local management support is also strongly influenced by the advocacy of senior management. Training specialists must show higher management that learning and performance outcomes will have a favorable effect on operating results. When higher management is convinced, support is usually forthcoming from subordinate managers, too.

The following sections describe the process used on a project that addressed each of the concerns discussed above. The project also illustrates collaboration of staff and line management to resolve an organizational performance problem.

The Problem

We faced a problem within a department of 5,000 employees who provided customers with service and equipment. Our management, like that of most businesses, was interested in improving productivity and performance quality. Management's objectives were being met in some geographical areas, but not in others. One executive was also concerned because performance objectives were set only for management employees. (The process used was similar to those described by Odiorne, 1961, and by Drucker, 1954). Since few nonmanagement employees were evaluated similarly, most were unaware of their own individual performance results and or their own contributions to service indices within the department. There were four populations to be dealt with—(1) nonmanagement technicians represented by a union, (2) their immediate supervisors, (3) area managers, and (4) middle managers.

We looked for symptoms contributing to the productivity-quality problem by interviewing personnel at all levels. We found the following conditions:

1. Technicians throughout the department were not all evaluated on the same dimensions of work.
2. Technicians were not always informed of expectations for quality and productivity unless they failed to meet them, nor were they commended for exceptional performance.
3. Technicians were not given appraisals of performance on a regularly scheduled basis.
4. Technicians' failure to meet expectations was usually countered by training or discipline (in the labor-relations sense).
5. First-level (immediate) supervisors were not trained in setting goals or appraising job performance.

From our data analysis, we sorted the causes of the problems into the same three types of deficiencies listed earlier. We then ranked the issues and devised a remedy addressing each deficiency. This remedy was installed in three phases.

Solutions

Performance-Improvement Strategy. Our first priority was to establish a departmental policy for setting objectives and appraising performance (within the terms of the union contract). This process included determining the minimum number of work dimensions to be used for measuring performance, the specific measurements to be monitored, and the minimum number of feedback sessions to be held between employees and supervisors.

We designed a program both to improve the work performance of technicians and to correct the inadequate and irregular appraisal system. We had found from experience that individual employees' performances were not greatly affected by employees' knowing their crews' results for productivity. One principle of our program, however, was that employees would improve more readily and take greater interest in results if they were informed of their own individual contributions to group indices (Maier, 1973).

Our program had several important characteristics. First-level supervisors were to perform the following actions with each technician:
- Establish desired performance levels, based on the person's ability, for every quarter and for the end of the year
- Monitor results
- Analyze deficiences
- Give quarterly feedback for good and poor performance
- Prepare action plans to overcome deficiencies.

Traditionally, punishment has been used to inhibit behavior instead of changing it (Maier, 1973). Supervisors were to develop action plans stating what employees must do, rather than what they must not do. A policy stipulated that these action plans must be devoid of disciplinary or any other language implying punitive consequences. Discipline was relegated to separate channels and could not be discussed in a session whose primary purpose was performance evaluation and development. We wanted to increase the probability of employees' accepting the action plans and thus changing their behavior.

The program included several other features. First, measurement and work standards for the technicians were selected from the same productivity and quality measurements on which their supervisors' performance objectives were set. Thus, our program underscored the need for subordinates' performances to be equal to or better than the performances specified by the supervisors' own performance objectives. Supervisors were encouraged to set work standards for technicians, so that, if these standards were met, the supervisors would also automatically meet their own objectives. Second, since the measurements to be monitored were standardized, paperwork was kept down: A single form was designed to accommodate the minimum requirements of the program, and space was left on it to let supervisors use it for additional measurements. Third, criteria for setting work standards were given, so that we could reduce instances of noncompliance among supervisors. Work standards had to be specific (stating the exact performance to be measured); individual (indicative of only one person's performance); quantitative (measurable and observable); realistic (set within the person's capability, yet challenging); and time-bound (expressed in a definite time frame for the employee to meet the standard). The quantitative nature of the work standards was stressed so that supervisors would become accustomed to evaluating performances on the basis of data, rather than according to their own likes or dislikes (Maier, 1973).

We also discouraged discussions of attitude, since such exchanges are usually pointless and do not accomplish what a supervisor intends: Employees tend to resent this subject, since they interpret the remarks as judgments on personality, character, and moral fiber. We believe that supervisors resort to this tactic when they wish to shift appraisal from the specific to the abstract (probably because they do not have all the facts). Rarely do such discussions end in positive remedies for changing either behavior or its associated attitudes. We believed that avoiding attitudinal evaluations would reduce unsubstantiated charges, confrontations, and conflicts about performance.

Finally, since this was an employee development program, unsatisfactory results were to be addressed by specific methods or activities for overcoming difficulties. For example, unsatisfactory workmanship would be treated with specific actions by the employee for improving quality. Similarly, basic satisfactory results were not to be recognized by external rewards, although superior performance was to be recognized, encouraged, and supported. We hoped employees would derive motivation from internal factors such as those described by Harzberg, Mausner, and Snyderman (1959).

Implementation Strategy. The program was introduced at a session for middle and senior managers. At that time, middle managers were instructed in training-delivery methods so that they could present information to their management teams. In this style, called family training, managers and supervisors within a common reporting area received training together. Since middle managers conducted the sessions with subordinates, they were able to demonstrate their own support for the program and to answer questions on policy and local requirements. Furthermore, the program was perceived as departmental rather than corporate, so that lower-level managers viewed it as directed toward their needs.

Middle managers held orientation sessions with their area managers. They explained the processes, benefits, and responsibilities associated with the program. These sessions were crucial to later acceptance by first-level supervisors. Area managers were the key personnel in the implementation process, since their enthusiasm and support would influence the degree to which the plan was followed as designed.

The training session included modules on procedures to be followed in the program. Three of the five allotted hours were devoted to practice exercises on setting work standards, developing action plans, and giving performance feedback. In addition, instruction was given on performance analysis, that is, matching appropriate solutions to deficiencies. This instruction was designed to highlight other remedies besides training or discipline. Middle managers were provided answer sheets that gave explanations for each correct and incorrect response to particular problems. Area managers at this session cited examples of action plans applicable to their own workplaces. We also observed the sessions, clarified procedures, gave suggestions for delivery improvements, and generally assisted whenever we could: We wished to ensure uniform application of both the training and the program.

The program was introduced to the technicians in individual meetings. We suggested that supervisors present information about the program to union stewards first, a courtesy that would allow stewards to respond to the union's members about the nature and intent of the program (company labor-relations managers already had inspected the plan and found it in compliance with the union contract).

Monitoring Strategy. Area and middle managers were responsible for overseeing the program on a continuous basis. The area managers were also required twice a year to review supervisors' forms and adherence to procedures. Middle managers were to review documents annually.

Within six months after introducing the program, we visited offices to review each supervisor's records. We gave feedback privately and provided tutoring when it was necessary. No information about specific individuals was given to the managers. This procedure was a break with convention, since most performance-improvement programs tend to be followed by audits, with negative consequences; our intent was to have the program seen as a valuable management technique.

Results

Supervisors have accepted the prescribed processes and are using the program as it was intended. To date, there have been no grievances associated with it. Preliminary data are encouraging. Improvements have been recognized in productivity and quality, although we must also acknowledge the influence of other factors on these results. At this writing, we have insufficient data to claim singular success on a long-term basis, but our data do indicate some favorable effects.

Discussion

This project dealt with a means for developing and maintaining good work habits among employees. Several methods were used. First, policy was established on the use of feedback. Second, supervisors were trained in setting work standards, in evaluating performance, and in giving feedback. Third, managers' participation was deemed integral to implementation and follow-up. Fourth, steps were taken to correct behavior, rather than punish it.

We believe that combining ideas from instructional technology and management practice is a key to the success of any performance-improvement system. The program described in this chapter will be extended to other work groups within our organization and could be appropriate in other settings, too. The philosophical elements of the program are not based solely on our own requirements. For instance, we believed work would improve if employees first were given standards in writing and then were informed of their own good, poor, or failed performance. Research has confirmed this conviction

(Latham and Yuki, 1975). We also believed that individual feedback would motivate employees to meet performance goals. The field results have supported our beliefs.

In the developmental stages of this project, some managers and supervisors expressed concern over the nonnegotiable nature of work standards. The literature (Tolchinsky and King, 1980) and our own findings, however, have shown us that assigned objectives, when handled carefully, can produce the desired improvements.

Projects like the one described here require trainer-managers to demonstrate flexibility and acceptance of work conditions. The performance problem must be understood in its true nature, as shown by the data. For example, if the problem is beyond the control of the employee, as in cases of poor administration, we must say so; it would be foolish to suggest training when the cause is not lack of skill or knowledge. Training persons to do what they already know how to do is a waste of time, manpower, and money.

We also must recognize our own predilections for one type of solution or another and adapt our preferences to meet the organization's needs. For example, if the corporate trainer has a special predilection for using audiovisual equipment, he or she may be tempted to use it inappropriately. Other predispositions are more subtle, but just as insidious, as in multistage solutions that are less effective than they might be because of overdependence on a specialist's philosophical prejudices. For example, a specialist inclined toward experiential approaches may select this strategy when a more structured approach would work better. Trainer-managers must use a repertoire of skills in balance with the problems at hand.

Finally, success must be judged by improvements in the conditions that called for training services in the first place. These improvements are often not immediate, since it takes time for new behaviors to become firmly established. To be perceived as useful within an organization, trainers must show not only what *they* can do but also what learner-employees can do.

Conclusions

We offer the following performance-improvement guidelines, based on an approach that combines attention to instruction as well as to supervision.
1. Analyze the work situation to understand causes of those problems that can be solved by education and training.
2. Select content relevant to the problem and that employees must master before a solution can occur.
3. To set clear and realistic educational objectives, specify the desired standards of performance.
4. Develop an educational strategy that fits the situation, not just the trainer's preferences.

5. Establish a schedule based on working conditions.
6. Allow employees time and opportunities to practice and achieve performance standards.
7. Monitor both the educational process and any changes in job performance.
8. Use evaluation to analyze progress and deficiences; provide feedback to correct instead of punish substandard performance; suggest needed adjustments.
9. Let education and training function as part of a broad performance-improvement effort.
10. Obtain support for education and training from supervisors and managers.

References

Bloom, B. S. (Ed.). *Taxonomy of Educational Objectives: The Classification of Educational Goals. Handbook I: Cognitive Domain.* New York: Longman, 1956.

Chellino, S. N., Rice, R. L., and Dinneen, M. "A Corporate Training Audit." Paper presented at annual conference of the National Society for Performance and Instruction, San Francisco, March 1978.

Drucker, P. F. *The Practice of Management.* New York: Harper & Row, 1954.

Gilbert, T. F. "Praexonomy: A Systematic Approach to Identifying Training Needs." *Management of Personnel Quarterly,* 1967, *6* (3), 20–33.

Harless, J. H. *An Ounce of Analysis (Is Worth a Pound of Objectives).* McLean, Va.: Guild Publications, 1970.

Harzberg, F., Mausner, B., and Snyderman, B. B. *The Motivation to Work.* New York: Wiley, 1959.

Latham, G. P., and Yuki, G. A. "A Review of Research on the Application of Goal-Setting in Organizations." *Academy of Management Journal,* 1975, *18,* 824–845.

Mager, R. F., and Pipe, P. *Analyzing Performance Problems (or You Really Oughta Wanna).* Belmont, Calif.: Fearon Press, 1970.

Maier, N. R. F. *Psychology in Industrial Organizations.* Boston: Houghton Mifflin, 1973.

Odiorne, G. S. *How Managers Make Things Happen.* Englewood Cliffs, N.J.: Prentice-Hall, 1961.

Smith, M. E., and Corbett, A. J. "Exchanging Ideas on Evaluation: 2. Basic Goals in Evaluating Post-Training Job Performance." *NSPI Journal,* 1976, *15* (7), 12.

Tolchinsky, P. D., and King, D. C. "Do Goals Mediate the Effects of Incentives on Performance?" *Academy of Management Review,* 1980, *5* (3), 455–467.

Susan N. Chellino is a trainer-manager with New England Telephone Company. Her primary responsibilities include instructional design and delivery for trainers, middle managers, and field supervisors. She also has held positions in training and line management. She is a doctoral candidate at Boston University.

Richard J. Walker is a manager with New England Telephone Company. He has had line and staff responsibilities, including both developing and teaching performance-improvement systems. Mr. Walker holds a B.B.A. degree from the University of Massachusetts.

Proprietary schools are educating more and more people every year. The Dale Carnegie organization's course is an example of some new aspects of adult education.

Change Strategies Used by a Proprietary School: The Dale Carnegie Organization

Paul J. Mackey

Proprietary schools have a variety of functions. They offer continuing professional education, vocational training, general self-improvement courses, and even courses devoted to increasing enjoyment of hobbies and personal interests. Recent developments that have created a climate in which the country's proprietary schools are thriving include recognition by accrediting associations, increased federal financial aid, increased need for the kinds of specific job training in which proprietary schools specialize, and the adoption by traditional colleges of advertising and marketing devices that were previously used only by proprietary schools (Maeroff, 1977).

Vocational Education

Many vocational schools and institutions exist to train individuals in a variety of proficiencies. The National Association of Trade and Technical Schools (NATTS) has published a pamphlet called *A Handbook of Trade and Technical Careers and Training* (NATTS, 1980), which presents a detailed national listing of over 500 schools accredited by this organization. Also listed are ninety-eight careers that can be learned in two years or less, as well as the schools that offer training for them. Figure 1 contains a list of the proficiency areas in which NATTS members offer courses, with listings of the length of time it takes to complete the courses.

At any one time, approximately 175,000 people are taking courses in these accredited proprietary schools, and about 105,000 graduate each year. (Many hundreds of thousands more are attending trade schools that are not listed because they are not accredited.) Trade and technical schools exist in practically every community in the country. Most individuals hear about them through the recommendations of others, but the schools also advertise in newspapers and on radio and television, as well as by direct mail. These schools are primarily independent, small establishments. Most are local, although some are part of national organizations. They often have fewer than 200 or 300 students. The instructors are almost always people employed in the fields in which they have studied. Most of these schools have a fairly good record of placing people in jobs.

Accreditation

The accreditation process is a lengthy one. A school usually has to have been operating successfully for a minimum of two years and must meet standards established by an accrediting commission. Proprietary trade and technical schools use NATTS as the accrediting body. According to the NATTS evaluation system, an accredited school must:
- Truthfully advertise its services
- Clearly set forth its enrollment terms
- Charge reasonable tuition
- Admit only qualified students
- Offer up-to-date courses
- Employ instructors experienced in their fields
- Maintain adequate equipment
- Keep classes to a reasonable size
- Provide guidance and placement services.

To ensure that these requirements are met, members of the accreditation team visit classrooms and observe instructors, examine equipment, solicit evaluations from students, and listen to any complaints students may have. The team also checks with the Better Business Bureau and other consumer organizations to discover whether complaints have been registered against the school and what actions have been taken.

Certification of Completion

All proprietary schools issue some type of certificate to graduates. Some schools are authorized by their state governments to issue associate

Figure 1. Skill Training Available at Accredited Schools

SKILL	TERM
Acting	150 weeks
Air Conditioning	12–73 weeks
Art, Commerical	52–136 weeks
Art, Fine	104–152 weeks
Appliance Repair	12–72 weeks
Architectural Engineering Technology	60–100 weeks
Automotive Mechanics	14–50 weeks
Aviation Mechanics	33–84 weeks
Baker	18 weeks
Barber/Hairstylist	32–52 weeks
Blueprint Reading	3–40 weeks
Brickmasonry	102 weeks
Broadcaster	13–48 weeks
Broadcasting Technician	10–92 weeks
Building Maintenance	52–60 weeks
Camera Service and Repair	16–50 weeks
Carpentry	102 weeks
Civil Engineering Technolgoy	18–104 weeks
Coin-operated Machine Repair	26 weeks
Computer Service Technician	30–120 weeks
Construction Technology	32–104 weeks
Dance Instructor	64 weeks
Data Processing	21–100 weeks
Dental Assisting	12–50 weeks
Dental Laboratory Technician	26–72 weeks
Diamond Cutting and Grading	26–40 weeks
Diesel Mechanics	10–38 weeks
Dietetics	13–52 weeks
Diving	8–15 weeks
Drafting	17–88 weeks
Dress Making and Design	3–88 weeks
Electricity	21–104 weeks

SKILL	TERM
Electrology	52 weeks
Electronics	24–108 weeks
Emergency Medical Technician	28–34 weeks
Engraving	12 weeks
Fashion Design	33–96 weeks
Fashion Illustration	52–136 weeks
Fashion Merchandising	5–74 weeks
Floral Design	10 weeks
Food Service	52 weeks
Gemologist	26 weeks
Gunsmithing	69 weeks
Heating	12–24 weeks
Heavy Equipment Operator	3–10 weeks
Horsemanship	11–38 weeks
Horticulture	40 weeks
Hotel-Motel Training	15–16 weeks
Illustration	136 weeks
Industrial Management	72 weeks
Inhalation Therapy Technician	37–52 weeks
Instrument Maker/Repairer	16 weeks
Instrumentation	78–80 weeks
Interior Design	64–108 weeks
Jewelry Design	12–40 weeks
Legal Secretarial/Asst.	24–52 weeks
Locksmith	10 weeks
Loss Prevention/Security	16 weeks
Machine Shop	14–102 weeks
Makeup Artist	8 weeks
Mechanical Engineering Technology	64–108 weeks
Medical Assistant	12–43 weeks
Medical/Dental Receptionist	16–27 weeks

Source: NATTS, 1980.

degrees. Proprietary schools that issue associate degrees must meet the standards established in their states.

Faculty Members

Most faculty members of proprietary trade schools are not college-trained educators; their experience in the field constitutes their teaching credentials. Many of the schools offer in-service education in teaching techniques, while others do not, depending instead on the personal talents of individual faculty members. More and more proprietary schools are hiring people who have studied education in college and have taught in elementary or high schools. Many schools also hire their own graduates as teachers. This practice is particularly valuable, because these graduate-teachers are well aware of the school's teaching techniques and have also had several years of field experience since graduation. Most of these schools hire only part-time teachers. This practice is generally an advantage for both the students and for the school, since an instructor working in the field can talk about or demonstrate things that have occurred that very day on the job.

Dropouts

NATTS-accredited schools have an average dropout rate of about 35 percent. This figure includes students dismissed for disciplinary or academic reasons, those who accepted employment before graduation, and those who left for such personal reasons as illness, marriage, pregnancy, or financial problems (Herbert and Coyne, 1980).

Curriculum

The curriculum differs in each school according to the philosophy of administrators. Some curricula are very structured and uniform while others are flexible. Most courses involving manual skills provide laboratory or shop facilities as the crux of the course, and much class time is spent in the lab or shop. Many schools also have arrangements with local companies to provide work/study programs. These programs allow students to spend part of their class time on the job. Thus, they get additional laboratory or shop work, as well as theoretical background. In short, according to Herbert and Coyne (1980), "most schools do what they promise to do: train people for the best possible job performance in the shortest amount of time."

How Good Are the Trade Schools?

According to one large study conducted by the American Institute for Research, more than 80 percent of all students surveyed said that their schools "provided good job training, practical skills emphasis, good teaching, and equipment needed for learning" (NATTS, 1980). The majority of the students complete their training in six to twelve months, while 65 to 75 percent will graduate; 60 to 68 percent will get jobs directly related to their training, a high percentage, considering that, in any group of young people, some do not want to go to work immediately, some do not do well in interviews, and some have barely passed their courses.

The Dale Carnegie Organization and the Dale Carnegie Course

In addition to vocational courses, proprietary schools also may offer courses that are concerned with self-improvement and self-development. One of the pioneers in such courses is the Dale Carnegie organization, whose programs have been presented in various forms since 1912. Over two million people have graduated from these courses, and over 105,000 people continue to enroll each year. The Dale Carnegie courses are offered in sixty countries, as well as in every major city in the United States.

The Dale Carnegie course in Effective Speaking and Human Relations was originally designed by Dale Carnegie himself. It has retained its success over the years because it has delivered what it promises. People enroll in this course to develop more self-confidence, enhance their personal philosophies, communicate more effectively, and improve their interpersonal skills. The completion rate worldwide for this course is over 85 percent, considerably higher than the completion rate for most courses offered in proprietary schools.

Accreditation. The Dale Carnegie organization is accredited by the Council for Noncollegiate Continuing Education, organized in 1974 as the Continuing Education Council. This body is committed to improving continuing education through accreditation, consultation, publication, research, conferences, and workshops. It primarily services the private and nonprofit sectors, as well as organizations having no other access to accreditation.

This council has established standards for accrediting continuing education programs in the broad noncollegiate field. Its procedures closely follow those of other nationally recognized accrediting agencies. It is governed by a board of directors chosen from among members of the council. Its national headquarters are in Richmond, Virginia. The council's accrediting commission is listed by the U.S. Commissioner of Education as a nationally recognized accrediting agency.

Who Was Dale Carnegie? Born on a farm in Missouri, Dale Carnegie attended the State Teachers College at Warrensburg. In 1912, he began to teach public speaking at the 125th Street YMCA in New York City. Enrollments in his courses soon spread to Boston and Washington, and Carnegie became a "glorified circuit-rider," teaching in the cities within that geographical area.

Throughout his active career as an adult educator, Carnegie experimented with new approaches and accepted those that furthered his objectives. He was influenced by the pragmatism and functionalism of John Dewey's learn-by-doing philosophy. Carnegie believed that adults learn best by being involved in the learning process, and he rejected the traditional lecture approach to teaching, since he thought lectures offer no assurance that learning is taking place. His book, *How to Win Friends and Influence People*, was published in 1936. The phenomenal sales of the book brought him into international prominence, and his course spread all over the country and to many foreign lands.

Pedagogical Approach. People enrolled in the Dale Carnegie Course are constantly urged to participate. Participation ranges from personal talks and reports to group exercises, role playing, and group discussions. Individuality is emphasized early: Class members are encouraged to compare themselves at any point in the course with themselves when they began the course, but not with other class members. This emphasis helps prevent feelings of inferiority among participants. The instructor also confers with class members about the progress they have made. A class member's goals are defined in the early sessions, and the instructor strives to reinforce these goals in each of the fourteen class meetings, pointing out how each session contributes to individual progress.

Attitude conditioning is an important part of instructional strategy. For this reason, course benefits are constantly emphasized as a way of encouraging participation. In comments the instructor makes after a participant's talk or report, specific mention is made of progress toward individual goals. For instance, a class member may have expressed a desire to deal more effectively with coworkers as one reason for taking the course. After a report in which the class member describes how he applied one of the human relations principles, the instructor may comment, "It is obvious that George showed real sensitivity toward the feelings of others on his staff in this particular situation. He is doing something about improving his leadership abilities, and this is moving him toward the objectives he told us he had established for himself when he first enrolled in the course." Then the instructor will address George directly: "We are glad that these positive experiences are beginning to happen to you more consistently. They are happening because you are making them happen through your own initiative." This comment reinforces the class member's motivation to continue modifying his behavior toward others, maintaining an attitude of acceptance, and taking the initiative to build more constructive interpersonal relationships. This instructional strategy is also consonant with the principles of "andragogy" espoused by Knowles (1972, p. 110).

The Dale Carnegie Course instructors strive to be positive, encouraging, approving, and optimistic about achievement. Instructors also attempt to improve class members' capacities on the spot, in situations rich in potential for improvement. After each talk or report, a very brief comment—often just one or two sentences—tells the class member and the entire class the accomplishment made at that moment. Sometimes the reinforcement even takes the form of an intervention for a few seconds in the middle of the talk. Dale Carnegie course instructors call this type of immediate reinforcement *coaching* or *drill*. Coaching and drill serve the psychological principle of recency that Thorndike, Skinner, and others have proposed. This principle is the heart of Dale Carnegie instruction, for it is on this basis that the learning process comes to life and class members become aware of their own progress and growth.

If class members learned only in the classroom and did not carry their learning into their lives, the Dale Carnegie Course would not be unusual. Instructors are responsible for influencing the class members to make sincere and meaningful application of the course to their own lives. The course is designed as a sequence of learning components, ranging from the simple to the complex; application comes before, during, and after sessions. For instance, a human relations principle may be discussed at one session, studied between sessions, put into practice before the next session, and reported on during the next session. As a result of the dynamics of that session, follow-through application should continue to occur. Gagné (1965, p. 26) agreed with this approach when he wrote that "teaching means the arranging of conditions that are external to the learner and which he is able to internalize into conditions for his individual learning."

Educational Philosophy. The educational philosophy behind the Dale Carnegie Course is basically eclectic; both practical and pragmatic means cantinue to be employed. Instead of psychological reasons for the processes that are followed, class members are given easily understood principles. For example, class members are told to select a subject they have earned the right to discuss, and which they are eager to talk about. People are self-confident and at ease when talking about familiar subjects. Class members are aware that their own experiences constitute a pragmatic basis on which to select a subject and release themselves to their own natural styles when discussing the subject with others.

While academic courses in public speaking devote considerable time to individual criticism on eye contact, posture, use of notes, and so forth, the Carnegie Course evaluates the speaker's ability to overcome fear and speak with sincerity and enthusiasm. Since the Carnegie Course is primarily a course in self-development, public speaking is only a vehicle to help class members master situations. The Carnegie philosophy is that if emphasis is placed on specific parts of a talk, rather than on the whole talk or on the speaker, then the student speaker will be left with a series of discrete comments on trivial matters, but will learn very little about the real situation. By recognizing and concentrating on the whole situation instead of on its components, the Carnegie instructor leaves class members with positive reactions.

Dale Carnegie's writings contain many references to William James and John Dewey, whose work he undoubtedly found inspiring. He also thought Émile Coué's theory of autosuggestion had a place in the Carnegie Course. Coué theorized that a person's "inward conversation" determined his overt actions. If a person tells himself, "I'm a failure," then he will be a failure. If, however, the person tells himself that he is a success, that he is improving, that he is getting better and better, then he will tend to become more successful.

Instructional Techniques. From the beginning, Carnegie Course enrollees are encouraged by their instructors' comments and by the approval (applause) of other class members. No one is permitted to return to his or her seat after a talk without experiencing a feeling of accomplishment. This feeling is reinforced by the other speakers: When class members see that others are successful, they tend to become more self-confident, too. In several sessions, class members are also taught to give themselves pep talks before getting up in front of the group. Many participants report that they also give themselves pep talks before engaging in any other major activity: Salesmen give themselves pep talks before visiting new prospects; employees give themselves pep talks before asking for raises; and athletes give themselves pep talks before crucial plays.

In each of the fourteen weekly sessions, every member of the class participates once and sometimes two times by talking before the group, either on prepared topics or impromptu. Instructors' remarks and comments are limited, not to exceed one minute. Each session is divided into two segments. The first segment is usually fast-moving, giving everyone an opportunity to present a short talk as a warmup.

Speaking assignments are based on the life experiences of class members. This practice also affords learners insight into their own development and motivations. The listening class members become aware of similarities in the experiences being related. They begin considering themselves more positively; they are less fearful in certain situations, and thus fear loses its significance. Class members also note the value of applying the course principles as speakers give solid evidence of how the principles can work to benefit them in their own jobs or at home. Knowles has written (1973, p. 43), "In the last decade a new, coherent, comprehensive body of theory and technology has been emerging, based on assumptions about adults as learners. We are beginning to absorb into our culture the ancient insight that the heart of education is learning, not teaching, and so our focus has started to shift from what the teacher does to what happens to the learner."

Present-Day Influences. The ideas of humanistic psychologists such as Rogers, Maslow, Fromm, and May are being integrated into the educational philosophy of the Dale Carnegie organization. More emphasis is being placed on learners' self-assurance and self-acceptance. From the field of adult education, the writings of Knowles, Houle, Kempfer, Tough, Kidd, and Lindemann are also influencing the staff programs. The course content and methods of instruction are constantly being reviewed to ensure that they reflect not only the latest thinking in adult education but also the human potential movement, which has been emerging since World War II, and of which the Dale Carnegie Course was a forerunner.

Summary

According to the National Center for Education Statistics, more than 21,000,000 persons seventeen years of age and older participate in adult education each year. This figure represents almost 13 percent of the total adult population of the United States. Educators estimate that there are well over a million students in as many as ten thousand proprietary schools throughout the country, and this fact makes proprietary schools relevant to new directions in continuing education.

References

Gagné, R. *The Conditions of Learning.* New York: Holt, Rinehart & Winston, 1965.
Herbert, T., and Coyne, J. "Getting Skilled." In *A Guide to Private and Technical Schools.* New York: Dutton, 1980.
Knowles, M. S. "Approaches in Teaching Styles and Approaches Based on Adult Learning." *Journal of Education for Special Work,* 1972, *8* (2), 110.
Knowles, M. S. *The Adult Learner: A Neglected Species.* Houston: Gulf Publishing, 1973.
Maeroff, G. I. "Profitmaking Schools Gain in Status." *New York Times,* September 11, 1977, Section D, p. 40.
National Association of Trade and Technical Schools (NATTS). *A Handbook of Trade and Technical Careers and Training.* National Association of Trade and Technical Schools, 1980.

Paul J. Mackey is vice-president of instruction at Dale Carnegie & Associates, Garden City, New York.

Two-year institutions use extensive local contacts to provide realistic educational experiences organized around behavioral objectives.

Effective Occupational Programs at Technical and Community Colleges

James J. Corbett

This chapter is concerned primarily with the postsecondary programs at technical and community colleges. Since their founding, these institutions have steadfastly maintained their original educational philosophies and integrity, although a gradual change in emphasis, from production and management to the more technical aspects of related business and industry, has also taken place. During this transition, these institutions have been ever alert to adapt their offerings to the changing needs of individuals interested in vocational careers.

These two-year institutions are designed to prepare high school graduates for entry-level technical or semiprofessional positions in their chosen occupational fields, while also providing a foundation for those students who wish to continue their education.

More than 25 million Americans have less than an eighth-grade education. For many of them, a return to the classroom, often fraught with memories of failure, can be more threatening than staying in a dead-end job for lack of skills. To help these undereducated adults face returning to the classroom, the Research Triangle Institute's Center for Educational Research and

S. M. Grabowski (Ed.). *Strengthening Connections Between Education and Performance.* New Directions for Continuing Education, no. 18. San Francisco: Jossey-Bass, June 1983.

Evaluation in North Carolina began experimenting with a new version of a technique called the Personalized System of Instruction (PSI) to teach adults basic skills (Wexler, 1980, p. 29).

Occupational education has been developed, refined, and funded over the years. Some occupational education programs are now threatened by budget cuts or by lack of understanding on the part of the power structure. At such times, it is important to come to occupational education's defense.

The purpose of such education is to provide not only the understanding of work techniques but also an appreciation of work's fundamental role in sustaining the values of our society. It is essential to recognize that there are members of our society who are ill equipped to benefit from the coming of the information age—indeed, who are ill equipped to survive day-to-day life. For example, according to Barron and Kelso (1975), 15 to 25 percent of Americans over eighteen are unable to manage their own lives. This is because they cannot comprehend the intellectual tasks required for day-to-day living. Furthermore, studies suggest that perhaps an additional third of our population is only marginally competent in these same skills (Swanson, 1981).

In occupational education, students are given recognition as individuals and guided toward their best achievements in all activities. Courses are supplemented to meet special interests and needs, and all students are encouraged to participate in those out-of-class programs that will help them develop their potentials and give them full expression. Hence, the student's total educational experience is a motivating force toward continuing personal and occupational growth, culminating in greater contributions to family, community and country (Duncan and Vess, 1971).

Occupational education throughout the years has always had the dual goals of education and community service. Today, it is a multiservice type of education serving the needs of full-time postsecondary students, as well as of part-time day and evening students. The offerings range from one-day seminars to two-year programs.

This type of education prepares students to become wage earners in the community by providing them with opportunities to learn practical, useful skills. It provides opportunities for more advanced education both in state-of-the-art technologies and in marketable skills. Occupational and technical training are seen as effective approaches to education for a segment of the population. Many adults seek out two-year technical and community colleges that are vocationally oriented and geared toward meeting immediate goals (Pifer, 1974). These two-year institutions generally allow students to use hands-on learning experiences and continue working at the same time.

The objectives of occupational education for technical and community colleges are to meet the needs and interests of the following groups:

- Those who are currently employed and desire additional education

- Those who want to enrich their backgrounds through specially designed courses or to pursue leisure interests.
- Those who enjoy lectures, forums, minicourses, concerts, film festivals, short-term workshops, institutes, seminars, and so forth (Cotoia, 1973, p. 1).

The potential for occupational education is great; it keeps changing with the times, so that today community technical colleges offer more than 14,000 occupational education programs, and there are more on the way (Harper, 1972, p. 12). The needs of society are being met by community technical colleges that offer such courses as meat inspection, hotel management, health science, marine science, textile industry skills, and many other courses that reflect local manpower needs.

Occupational education prepares students for the world of work after they graduate, partly because students not only attend classes but also obtain employment in related job areas during the school year. The fundamental promise of occupational education is to make relevant learning available to young people who are confronted by changing social and economic requirements (Marland, 1972). Accordingly, these two-year institutions:

- Prepare qualified people for satisfying and profitable careers as owners, managers, supervisors, technicians, sales-and-service personnel, or skilled specialty workers in the specific occupational fields for which they have been trained
- Provide opportunities through program experience and guidance, which both encourage continuing balanced growth of personality and cultural competencies
- Provide basic education sufficient to allow graduates to continue their education at the college level
- Provide short courses and programs for keeping participants up-to-date in new management practices, changes in technology, and research findings, with added background for problem recognition and decision making (Archambault, 1977).

Some institutions also maintain cooperative extension services to:

- Assist individual farmers, horticulturalists, and people in related businesses by providing information and economic guidance
- Provide needed instruction and service in improved family and community living
- Aid communities and public service organizations in cooperative projects leading to public betterment (Archambault, 1977).

A community college is a very exciting environment in which to work. The atmosphere is very conducive to learning, and a person's voice is generally heard. Thanks to flexible admissions policies, low cost, and a broad mix of educational offerings community and technical colleges can take considerable credit for expanding the base of education beyond high school for minorities.

Curriculum

In two-year institutions, curriculum development and implementation are particularly important in terms of students' ability to perform on the job. There are at least six curriculum determinants other than the individual instructor: Other institutions, the community, the institution, the faculty, the department, and the students all help select and shape what is taught in the technical community college (Whiteley, 1971). A great deal of planning, organization, evaluation, and feedback goes into the development process to make occupational education programs more relevant to the needs of the marketplace and of the community.

Occupational education offers us the distinct advantage of being able to use many different sources for decisions. We can talk with and listen to people in business, industry, and schools; instructors; local citizens; and students. Occupational education is unique, since its curriculum is shaped by the business community, as well as by educators. Department chairpersons also influence curriculum development, and they provide additional help to faculty members with regard to updating curricula.

In occupational education, a well-developed curriculum requires us to know the community, be sure of our objectives, plan activities for work and school, and use as many new educational techniques as possible. In practice, teachers often tailor subject matter to the needs of particular students (Gordon and Solmon, 1981).

Specific proposals for alternatives to formal education programs include extended campuses, special adult degrees, individualized study, external degree programs, summer school, educational passports, continuing education units, and provision of educational leave from jobs (Gordon and Solmon, 1981). Each one of these proposals lends itself quite easily to occupational and continuing education programs.

Many technical colleges use a modified form of management by objectives (MBO) to ensure students' attainment of proficiences. MBO singles out certain activities for emphasis in class; it is now part of the federal-state-local system of vocational-technical education (Mager, 1962).

In this era of technological expertise, industrial educators must adopt some type of pedagogical system (Yankelovich, 1972). The same thing can be said about all occupational educators. Once instructors have identified behavioral objectives based on a rationale for the concept to be taught, content and related activity can be structured to fit the system's needs (Goodman, 1972). A learning environment is established through the interaction of behavioral objectives and the curriculum.

Technical education is a specialized category of two-year education. It prepares students for jobs in which some manual skills are required, but in which technical knowledge is emphasized (Buckholtz, 1981). Technical colleges nurture an almost symbiotic closeness with manufacturers and producers: Employers depend on technical colleges to provide skilled workers, while the colleges count on business and industry to hire their graduates (Buckholtz, 1981).

The Classroom

The instructor's role is primarily to provide required supplementary instruction, keep records, monitor materials, and give intensive instruction to the few students who do not have the skills necessary to begin a PSI unit (McCabe, 1972). Instruction is enhanced when instructors adhere to the following vocational principles:
1. The standards of the job should be the standards of the classroom.
2. First develop those proficiencies directly related to job success, and postpone the development of proficiencies an employer might consider "desirable" or simply "nice to know."
3. Developing individuals as total employees is a way of recognizing the demands of the contemporary job market, in which skills alone are insufficient (Haines and Mason, 1972).

It is estimated that 40 million adults in America will be making a career change in the next ten years. Of these, 24 million will turn to community colleges. These adults will enroll as part-time, employed students seeking specific courses and skills (Oliver, 1965). As more and more people have more leisure time, continuing education may also help people use their leisure time constructively.

We need to redefine our basic aims in education. Four related but distinct purposes that define comprehensive education can be specified:
- Identification of the talents and preferred learning styles of individuals
- The communication of physical and social knowledge about the world
- Development of the proficiencies needed to promote productivity and creativity
- Sharing values (Renberg, 1971).

Conclusions

The following guidelines indicate some of the many influences on the quality and impact of community college occupational education.
1. Recognize the importance of a strong and generalized commitment by community colleges and technical institutes to continuing education and community service.

2. Use extensive local contacts to know the community and respond to local needs.
3. Provide realistic educational experiences that benefit from the perspectives of part-time participants and instructors.
4. Have job standards serve as standards for educational programs.
5. To enhance proficiencies, emphasize educational activities that focus on behavioral objectives.
6. Remember that education depends largely on able instructors and well-designed programs.

References

Archambault, L. *College Handbook.* Hathorne, Mass.: Essex Agricultural and Technical Institute, 1977.
Buckholtz, M. "Keeping Up With a Revolution." *American Education,* 1981, *17* (9), 10-14.
Cotoia, A. M. *End of Year Report for the Division of Continuing Education and Community Service.* Beverly, Mass.: North Shore Community College, 1973.
Duncan, W. J., and Vess, D. M. "The 4-1-4 Academic Year." *Collegiate News and Views,* 1971, *24* (3), 9.
Fontelle, G. (Ed.). *Minorities and Community Colleges.* Washington, D.C.: American Association of Community and Junior Colleges, 1979.
Goodman, L. V. "Philander Claxton's Pet Idea." *American Education,* 1972, *8* (2), 1.
Gordon, J. J., and Solmon, L. C. *The Characteristics and Needs of Adults in Postsecondary Education.* Lexington, Mass.: Heath, 1981.
Haines, P. G., and Mason, P. E. *Cooperative Occupational Education and Work Experience in the Curriculum.* Danville, Ill.: The Interstate Printers & Publishers, 1972.
Harper, W. "This Way to the Jobs." *American Education,* 1972, *8* (2), 12-19.
McCabe, M. "Highlight Review for Store Managers." *The New NEGM Magazine,* 1972, *40* (11), 16.
Mager, R. F. *Measuring Instructional Objectives.* Belmont, Calif.: Lear Siegler, 1962.
Marland, S. P. "Career Education and the Two-Year Colleges." *American Education,* 1972, *8* (2), 11.
Oliver, A. I. *Curriculum Improvement.* New York: Dodd, Mead, 1965.
Pifer, A. "Community College and Community Leadership." *Community and Junior College Journal,* 1974, *44* (5), 23-24.
Renberg, T. "Education By Endurance." *The Deca Distributor,* 1971, *25* (3), 8-10.
Swanson, G. I. (Ed.). *The Future of Vocational Education.* Arlington, Va.: The American Vocational Association, 1981.
Wexler, H. "A Second Try at Basic Education." *American Education,* 1980, *16* (9), 29.
Whiteley, T. *The Elements of Curriculum Development.* Toronto: Ontario Institute for Studies in Education, 1971.
Yankelovich, D. "The New Naturalism." *The Saturday Review,* April 1, 1972, p. 37.

James J. Corbett is assistant professor of marketing at Merrimack College, North Andover, Massachusetts. Previously, he taught at Essex Agricultural and Technical Institute in Danvers, Massachusetts, and at North Shore Community College in Beverly, Massachusetts.

In the armed services, the differences between training and education have implications for training evaluation.

Military Education and Training

Gordon Larson

The Department of Defense operates the largest adult education enterprise in the country (Brodsky, 1970). In addition to training for combat skills, the military provides postservice educational opportunities throughout the world to veterans and their dependents. Given not only the magnitude and expense of military education and training but also constant political pressure to reduce military spending, the armed services are committed to obtaining maximum effectiveness from their training programs. This chapter examines how the services design, deliver, and evaluate these programs. Most of the discussion focuses on education and training in the Army, since the author has had the most experience with that service branch. Nevertheless, the basic training systems in all of the branches of the service are similar. Thus, the information provided in this chapter is generally applicable to all branches.

Understanding of how the military provides for effectiveness in its education and training programs is helped by an examination of the values by which effectiveness is measured. For example, both business and the military relate instructional effectiveness to increased performance: The "bottom line" for business is profit, while for the military the "payoff" is military readiness. Military readiness is thought to be achieved by acquiring and maintaining modern arms and equipment and by recruiting and training highly qualified and motivated personnel to operate it. Education and training both play important roles in readiness, but these roles are neither identical nor equivalent.

The Role of Training in the Military

To a civilian educator, the distinction between education and training may be largely philosophical, but in the military the difference between these two activities is significant. Training is the major peacetime activity of military leaders (U.S. Department of the Army, 1982), while education plays a supporting role. Training and education in the military also are controlled and conducted by entirely different agencies.

Military training, covering a broad scope of skills, includes subject matter ranging from rifle marksmanship to interracial dynamics to leadership skills. Current military goals dictate instructional objectives, while instructional content is determined by current military doctrine. In the Army, supervision by the Training and Doctrine Command (TRADOC) ensures uniform doctrine and training through this service branch. As General Donn A. Starry, a recent commander of TRADOC, has said (1979, p. 2), doctrine and training together constitute "the cement that bonds tactics, organizations, equipment, and soldiers into successful battle teams. If training is successful, readiness is the result." Similar concepts guide planning in all the other service branches.

Since training is based on goals as well as on doctrines, the basis for judging its effectiveness is its direct impact on individual or unit performance in achieving those goals. Before we consider how the military links operational and instructional objectives, let us examine the role of general education in the military.

The Role of Education in the Military

As Welling and others (1979, p. 1) have observed, "training and education... are designed to have complementary objectives. The basic objective of the Army Training System is to produce a combat-ready Army through the development of job performance skills. The Army Continuing Education System is geared toward meeting the soldier's personal educational and vocational goals...." This complementary role is apparent in the objectives of the Army Continuing Education System (ACES), which include keeping the Army ready for combat, attracting and retaining qualified personnel, and providing education to help them develop career goals that may include additional military service (U.S. Department of the Army, 1979, p. 1). Thus, while training is expected to provide a direct and immediate effect on military readiness, education's impact on readiness is more indirect.

The ACES staff consists primarily of Department of the Army civilians, since virtually all instruction is arranged through civilian educational agencies via tuition assistance plans or as on-post programs. The latter are conducted after normal duty hours.

Participation in the military's general education programs is usually voluntary. The military exerts little or no control over types and content of courses, and, for the most part, academic freedom is rigorously maintained. The military occasionally works with local educational agencies to develop specialized curricula for specific target groups within the service branches. For example, at Fort Dix the Army worked with a local college in 1976 to develop an associate degree program for drill sergeants. But programs like this one are exceptional; the military seldom plays a significant role in developing educational programs and is therefore relatively unconcerned about any immediate effects of education on military readiness. Education generally is viewed as a personnel benefit, and its effectiveness is assessed on the basis of its ability to attract and retain quality personnel.

As a major exception to this general description of the military's educational programs, basic skills education, a hybrid of training and education provided by all services, prepares inadequately educated enlisted personnel for participation in military training (McGoff and Harding, 1974). This is one case in which the military has taken an active role in designing and developing specific instruction to meet training needs (Sticht, 1975; Sticht and others, 1977; U.S. Army Training and Doctrine Command, 1979). For this reason, military monitoring of basic skills programs has been more thorough than for other kinds of instruction (U.S. Department of the Army, 1965; McGoff and Harding, 1974; Larson, 1979). Basic skills instruction is conducted during normal working hours, and attendance is mandatory for personnel requiring remediation; thus, much of what has been said about training also applies to basic skills education.

As discussed above, educational effectiveness is normally evaluated differently from training effectiveness. While training is by far the more important daily concern of commanders, education is still perceived as generally beneficial, so long as it does not interfere with normal operational requirements. Given this difference, the remainder of this chapter will concern itself primarily with training.

The Army Training System

The Army training system is typical of training systems in all the service branches. It provides for the military education of all soldiers, from basic training for enlisted recruits to the war college for aspiring general officers, as well as for the development of proficiencies at all organizational levels. Let us first examine individual training, as it applies to most enlisted personnel.

An enlisted person's career starts at the reception station, where soldiers are processed into the Army, issued their uniforms, and given their first indoctrination into military service. After a few days, the soldiers are sent to basic training, where they are given instruction in those military skills common to all soldiers, regardless of occupational specialty. Following basic training, most soldiers go immediately to advanced individual training, where they receive basic instruction in individual military specialties (in some cases, basic training and advanced individual training are combined). The Army provides entry-level training in more than 200 of its 345 occupational specialties at twenty-two training installations throughout the United States. Upon completion of entry training, soldiers report to their first duty assignments. At this point, training is integrated into other operational activities by means of locally developed training schedules. Soldiers in each occupational specialty follow a set of training requirements established by TRADOC. These standardized requirements are published in occupational specialty manuals developed to plan training as well as evaluate training and proficiency (U.S. Department of the Army, n.d.). First-line supervisors maintain job books to keep track of each soldier's ability to perform the crucial tasks listed in the manual. Tests are administered annually to ensure achievement of the necessary skills. The job books are also used to provide training-proficiency information to the higher command levels. Performance on the annual tests is used for individual promotion, and the overall results may also be used by commanders to manage unit training programs.

For career-oriented soldiers, the Army provides additional schooling in leadership skills, as well as in advanced occupational skills. Leadership skills are developed through the Non-Commissioned Officers Education System, while advanced occupational skills may be obtained either through temporary assignment to resident courses offered by various technical schools or through correspondence courses offered by the Institute for Professional Development.

In addition to individual training, soldiers participate in unit training, from the squad and crew levels to the battalion level and even higher levels. For example, tank gunnery training prepares tank crews to engage a variety of enemy targets with maximum effectiveness in the least possible time. Tank gunnery training involves eight levels of difficulty and complexity, called *tables,* culminating in a test of all crew skills. During this test, crews engage a series of targets while negotiating a prescribed course. The crews are evaluated for speed as well as for accuracy in using all the tank weapons systems.

Training Design

Effective training must be systematically designed. Instructional objectives must be clearly specified and directly related to some desired behavioral or attitudinal change. The military services have always exercised some degree of centralized control over training, and required training has always been related to percieved needs of the services, but only since the early 1970s has standardized instructional design been used by all the services. Under the old system, training requirements were specified in terms of a given number of hours of instruction to be undergone by all personnel. Mandatory requirements were specified at each level of command, based on commanders' perceptions of needs. At the unit level, where most training was conducted, a training sergeant would prepare a weekly training schedule, making sure to include a certain number of required classes each week, according to a master training schedule. Attendance was recorded, and the training sergeant would post attendance data on individual training cards. During his annual inspection, the inspector general would check all training schedules and spot-check individual training records to ensure that individual soldiers had received training. Units were evaluated according to how well they complied with requirements, including attendance requirements.

The actual effectiveness of training was seldom examined under the old system, except for skills in which proficiency was readily apparent, such as rifle marksmanship, or unless some incident brought attention to a given aspect of training. An example of the latter case occurred during the Pueblo crisis, when the sailors aboard the Pueblo violated some provisions of the Code of Conduct. The Code of Conduct, a required annual training subject for all service personnel, had been developed and taught to prevent the kinds of undesirable behavior that had occurred among prisoners of war in Korea. It was always assumed that personnel's knowledge of the code would be sufficient to regulate their behavior in similar situations, but the Pueblo incident dispelled that assumption and caused military commanders to re-evaluate the usefulness and effectiveness of the Code of Conduct training.

Under the new system, control over the training process is even more centralized and standardized, thanks to TRADOC. The design of training incorporates more front-end analysis of job and task requirements. Greater emphasis is placed on performance-oriented training and testing procedures, and less is placed on lectures and pencil-and-paper testing. Annual proficiency testing has also been modified to include a hands-on component designed to assess actual job-performance skills more accurately. The whole training system is geared to career development plans for each occupational specialty, specifying the skills required of soldiers at each grade level. Promotion is tied to performance on skills-qualification tests, and soldiers and their immediate supervisors are responsible for ensuring that the appropriate skills have been learned. In essence, training has been changed from a system based on clock-hour accountability to one based on proficiency.

To effect a change of this magnitude takes a long time, and some of the provisions of the new system are not yet fully implemented. Job analyses have been less than perfect in many cases, and there are always questions about which skills should be taught at what times. The hands-on component of the skills-qualification testing program also has been difficult to develop and implement, and it is not yet available for all specialties. Nevertheless, the new system has built greater accountability into military training and has undoubtedly increased training effectiveness.

Evaluation and Feedback

While the Army's skills-qualification tests assess whether individual training objectives have been met for each soldier in each occupational specialty, the Army Training and Evaluation Program is designed to achieve the same purpose for unit training. Each of the service branches has its own equivalent to these evaluation systems. The evaluation of military training effectiveness goes beyond formal analysis, however; the key to the effectiveness of military training is the close link between training and actual use of the skills learned.

Compared to the military, civilian educational agencies are at a disadvantage in obtaining feedback about the effectiveness of their programs; they must seek information from employers or from their alumni. They also must deal with variations in the conditions under which the knowledge and skills learned within an institution are applied in real-world settings. Both business and the military, in contrast, have the advantage of being users as well as providers of skills and, as organizations, are more able to evaluate the effectiveness of specific instruction systematically. The military, moreover, has an advantage over most business organizations in obtaining feedback on program effectiveness: In business, training departments must work with key personnel from the mainstream of the organization to obtain feedback, and the degree of cooperation they receive depends on the importance that line supervisors place on training. In the military, however, when training is not provided directly by line personnel, it is offered in training organizations staffed by line personnel only temporarily detailed as trainers. Thus, all trainers in the military eventually become users of their own products, and this arrangement not only creates a vested interest in training's effectiveness but also facilitates the flow of information between trainers and line supervisors outside the training establishment. Commanders of training units have close links with commanders in the field because of this rotation between field and training assignments. In this way, evaluation and feedback go on continuously and naturally within the military, and while attention to training may vary among individual units (depending on other operational requirements), the effectiveness of training programs is necessarily an important concern of the entire military system.

Summary

Education and training can contribute to military readiness, but the military never really knows how effective its training programs are until they are tested in combat. Otherwise, combat readiness tests and other evaluations of training effectiveness depend on the vision of leaders, who must anticipate the nature and conditions of potential confrontations.

Thus, the commitment of the military to continuing education is twofold. Optional educational activities not closely connected with military readiness are termed *education* and viewed as beneficial through the attraction and retention of high-quality personnel. By contrast, the term *military training* refers to competency-based educational activities, with operational objectives designed to have an impact on individual and unit performance. Guidelines for effective military training include continuity of training during the military career, task analysis as a basis of performance-oriented training, provision of a variety of training opportunities, training focused on the individual and on the team, use of sound educational design, evaluation of results in terms of improved performance that benefits the organization, and use of supervisors to provide training in which they themselves have a stake.

References

Brodsky, N. "The Armed Forces." In R. M. Smith, G. F. Aker, and J. R. Kidd (Eds.), *Handbook of Adult Education*. New York: Macmillan, 1970.

Larson, G. "Evaluating Military Literacy Programs." In A. B. Knox (Ed.), *Assessing the Impact of Continuing Education*. New Directions for Continuing Education, no. 3. San Francisco: Jossey-Bass, 1979.

McGoff, R. M., and Harding, F. D. *A Report on Literacy Training Programs in the Armed Forces*. Washington, D.C.: Office of the Assistant Secretary of Defense, Manpower and Reserve Affairs, 1974.

Starry, D. A. "Modernization of the Army: Issues to the Year 2000." Unpublished paper, 1979.

Sticht, T. G. *A Program of Army Functional Job Reading Training: Development, Implementation, and Delivery Systems*. Alexandria, Va.: Human Resources Research Organization, 1975.

Sticht, T. G., Fox, L. C., Hauke, R. N., and Zapf, D. W. *Integrated Job Skills and Reading Skills Training System*. San Diego, Calif.: Navy Personnel Research and Development Center, 1977.

U.S. Army Training and Doctrine Command. *Basic Skills Education Planning Group Executive Summary*. Fort Monroe, Va.: U.S. Army Training and Doctrine Command, 1979.

U.S. Department of the Army. *Marginal Man and Military Service: A Review*. Washington, D.C.: U.S. Department of the Army, 1965.

U.S. Department of the Army. *Army Continuing Education System*. Army Regulation 621-5. Washington, D.C.: U.S. Department of the Army, 1979.

U.S. Department of the Army. *How to Conduct Training in Units*. Field Manual 25-3 (draft). Washington, D.C.: U.S. Department of the Army, n.d.

U.S. Department of the Army. *How to Manage Training in Units.* Field Manual 25-2 (test). Washington, D.C.: U.S. Department of the Army, 1982.

Welling, J. R., Stock, J. R., Rossinger, G., Bridgman, M. S., and Myers, L. B. *Investigation of Approaches for Improving the Interface Between Army Education and Training.* Washington, D.C.: Department of the Army Adjutant General Center, 1979.

Gordon Larson is an assistant professor of adult education at Rutgers University. Previously, he spent fourteen years as an officer on active duty in the United States Army.

Education is a widely used practical tool in programming and can contribute to improved job performance.

Evaluation as a Guarantee of Performance in Cooperative Extension

Robert Lee Bruce

The basic process of evaluation—the elements involved and the relationships among them—is no different for cooperative extension than for any other organizational model. It may be described differently, and the diagrams depicting it may look different from those developed in other areas, but this difference derives from differences in terminology and from the tendency (as in other applied fields) to express general ideas in terms of their local analogues. The evaluation process, however, is basically the same. Nevertheless, because of the peculiar nature of cooperative extenstion, its reliance on single-use plans, and the fact that responsibility and authority for its program decisions involve so many different groups, it will be useful to consider its evaluation procedures as a separate branch of evaluation.

Organization of Cooperative Extension

Cooperative extension is neither a single program nor even a single program delivery system, but a complex of several systems working together. The word *cooperative* refers to cooperation among local, state, and federal governments in funding and managing extension programs.

The overwhelming majority of cooperative extension programs develop and operate locally in direct cooperation with the clientele groups they are intended to serve. While specific administrative structures at the local level vary, normally there is a high degree of local autonomy and clientele involvement, as well as a high level of local investment in terms of funding and volunteer leadership.

A state's role in a partnership is tested in the land-grant universities, where extension is a responsibility equal in importance to research and teaching. The universities provide program support and administrative direction, as well as coordination to let local programs take advantage of university resources. Such coordination also helps the universities serve local needs. The federal government provides funding and a limited amount of administrative and policy supervision through the Science and Education Administration of the United States Department of Agriculture (USDA).

The formal relationship among the partners is technically and theoretically one in which funding is provided in support of program proposals, and in which beneficiaries at each level are accountable for the use of resources and for accomplishing the goals expressed in the proposals. Several factors, however, interact to alter the actual nature of this relationship. One factor is the balance of resource support: Whatever the comparative dollars-and-cents contributions, when the in-kind services of university faculties and local leaders are considered, the system is locally oriented; thus, local programs can "go it alone," at least for limited periods. A second factor involves organizational traditions. There is a high level of commitment at all levels to accomplish local objectives as the ultimate criterion of success. A third factor is geography: The bulk of the professional staff is at the local level, in daily contact with (and thus accountable to) local people, who control vital resources and exert influence (United States Department of Agriculture, 1982).

Single-Use Plans

Like other organizational models for nonformal education, cooperative extension relies heavily on single-use plans. Instead of working through a curriculum that is repeated with only slight variations for successive groups of learners, extension tends to develop unique programs to deal with specific problems. Thus, the planning and implementation are likely to involve the full range of programming decisions.

In formal education, and in other areas where multiple-use plans dominate, decisions about objectives and even general methods are made early and reviewed rather infrequently. Furthermore, decisions are often made by people other than those who implement the program. Thus, practitioners are confined to program monitoring as a basis for making minor adjustments in curricula and plans, evaluating achievement (usually through testing students), and accounting to outside authorities (usually in terms of goal achievement).

In cooperative extension, however, personnel go through the entire programming process each time a program is developed. Various possible changes must be evaluated; objectives must be selected. Possible courses of action also must be considered, with the most suitable ones chosen. Even during program implementation, chosen methods must be monitored and program design altered as needed for maximum effect. Outcomes must be assessed as a basis for determining whether to recycle either program or audience, to terminate, or to move ahead. Finally, extension personnel must be accountable to far more diverse audiences than the ones formal educators must address.

Local Involvement

Cooperative extension is structured so that most of its staff members are in regular contact with the clientele, who are confronted daily with the consequences of its programming efforts. Local programs have direct control over many of their resources; often, especially in rural states, they are able to bring real pressure to bear on central administration personnel and on universities.

This structure has several consequences for program evaluation in cooperative extension. The first and most important one is a concern at the local level for practical outcomes. The programs' agents live among and are primarily responsible to their clients. Besides providing verbal feedback, clients are in a position to provide or withhold resources, salaries, and even job security. The local clients, however, are not the only audience to whom extension personnel are accountable. Despite the generally pragmatic democracy of the extension system, each of the cooperating levels has its own agenda. The USDA is the federal administrative body, charged with carrying out federal agricultural policy. The USDA is responsible both to the executive branch of government (to which it belongs) and to Congress, which provides its funds. Its support for state and local efforts is colored by these responsibilities, as are its evaluation efforts. The USDA, in turn, is another audience to which extension is accountable.

The state land-grant universities also have their own agendas. The increasing sophistication of their research has often been accompanied by greater specialization and sometimes also by declining interest in applied questions. Success in extension may be valued less by academically oriented faculties than is recognition from academic peers. Furthermore, dwindling funds and more sophisticated management on the part of state governments have led to the proliferation of long-range plans and mission statements that can be used to judge programming decisions. Since these statements define needs and thus suggest evaluation criteria—often based on academic ambitions, as well as on satisfying the needs of a broad extension audience—there is a source of potential conflict at this point.

Evaluation as a Practical Process

From the perspective of extension practitioners, evaluation is a tool for better decision making, rather than a technical exercise or an art form governed by tenuous rules. Since programming decisions are made at all levels and at all times, evaluation must not be regarded as a step in the programming process, but as an inseparable part of the whole process. Despite the fact that evaluation is pervasive, it is still only a tool for program improvement, not an end in itself; it must be kept practical. Of course, evaluation can be and often is used summatively—for self-congratulation, fixing blame, satisfying curiosity, or as a sort of low-grade research. Still, working organizations with objectives to attain cannot afford the luxury of superfluous evaluations. Evaluation must produce useful, timely, and cost-effective information.

Finally, we must recognize that evaluation has an inherent political dimension. Program decisions are made by human beings on the basis of criteria they accept as adequate grounds for their decisions. These criteria are seldom objective or absolute; they embody the wants and beliefs of those using them and are subject to challenge by other participants in the decision, or by those who will be affected. Such challenges are political and call for political solutions. Therefore, it will be useful to examine the decision settings in which evaluations occur and to have a look at the decision process itself.

The Decision Setting

In any program, four general kinds of decisions must be made (see Figure 1). Someone must decide which objectives are to be pursued. There must also be a preliminary selection of methods. With experience in the program come decisions about which aspects of the program process to keep or modify. Decisions must also be made about when to stop, repeat, or proceed. Stufflebeam (1971) has designated the evaluation processes associated with these decisions as *context, input, process,* and *product* evaluation processes.

Program management evaluations can be divided into three additional types, according to where decisions are made and whether the decision process is continuous or periodic. The most common decisions (in the literature, at least) are periodic decisions—that is, they occur at intervals during the programming process. There are also internal periodic evaluations, which are used inside the program and are often done by, or at the behest of, the program staff. Accountability evaluations are for use outside the program. Moni-

Figure 1. Programming Decisions and Evaluation Types

Program decision	Product	Evaluation type
What to try to accomplish	Objectives	Context Evaluation
How to go about accomplishing it	Initial Plan	Input Evaluation
Which methods to keep	Continuing plan	Process evaluation
When to stop, repeat, or go on		Product Evaluation

toring is an internal process that uses evaluation; it goes on continually (see Figure 2).

Context evaluations involve studying situations to decide which changes are needed and what ends to pursue. These evaluations can be made in general terms, or they may be very specific, occurring in stages. A state extension organization, for example, may conduct a context evaluation and arrive at a set of general objectives or program priorities that serve as a basis for additional programming. A county staff, working within that set of objectives, may do its own study and arrive at a more detailed set of priorities to guide individual agents in planning specific activities. These agents, in turn, may do their own detailed context evaluations.

In program monitoring, priorities derived from context evaluations serve as points of comparison. Still, an experienced and self-confident extension worker may also monitor the usefulness of objectives themselves. An objective that proves impossible or too costly to achieve, or even futile, may be modified, if not dropped.

Still another situation exists in accountability evaluation. This type of evaluation usually results from a kind of bargain, in which a resource (time, money, permission, and so on) is given in response to a proposal and the promise of results. In this case, the context evaluation that matters is the one on which the donor of resources acts (and in terms of which the proposal has been made and approved). The program staff may have additional objectives based on its own assessment, but it is the donor's assessment that matters.

Much the same thing can be said of input evaluation: In making the proposal for which resources were granted, the program staff makes decisions about what will or will not work. The donor, in accepting or rejecting the proposal, is also doing an input evaluation. In the case of monitoring, input evaluations are more likely to deal with modifications or methods—changes of pitch, emphasis, and speed—rather than with whole methods themselves (although this approach is not excluded). In every case, input evaluation

Figure 2. Management Evaluation

Locus of Decision	Periodic or Continuous	Types
Internal	Periodic	Internal Periodic
By program staff	Continuous	Monitoring
External By donor or other authority	Periodic At end of program of on fixed schedule	Accountability

involves basing decisions about methods and approaches on estimates of probable outcomes. These estimates may be based on previous experience.

Evaluating the utility of a process appears to differ from input evaluation, in that it looks back to our own experience. Having established or at least begun the program, we must ask how well it has worked and whether we should continue. There is, however, very little difference in the basic logic of the two evaluations. In each case, we are evaluating methods against objectives. More important, we are making estimates about future performance.

Even though a process evaluation may be based on past experience, it is about the future. We cannot change the past, but we can use it as a source of data on which to base decisions about what to do next. In monitoring situations, process and input evaluations are likely to be one and the same. In the case of accountability, the audience (the ultimate evaluator) may be evaluating not just the procedures used but also the program or organization using them, since choice of agency is also a method choice.

There is a second aspect of process evaluation—determining the extent to which plans have been followed—that is common to all three types of management evaluation. Donors contribute resources with the expectation that they will be used in particular ways, and donors may want to know that the resources have not been diverted to other uses. In addition, inside as well as outside evaluators need to know what was actually done to produce the results observed; otherwise, there is no sound basis for decisions about what will work in the future.

There is a great deal more to evaluation than measuring impact; nevertheless, product evaluation is central to most program decisions. Product evaluation goes beyond merely discovering whether or not objectives have been met. In all three types of management decision, judgments about process and recycling decisions alike depend on knowing not only whether objectives have been met, but also on knowing what planned or unplanned outcomes have occurred.

While all three evaluation types should take unplanned outcomes into account, such outcomes are especially important in monitoring. In other types of evaluation (and, to some extent, in monitoring), the basic logic is deductive: Evaluation problems are identified, criteria are set, indicators are deduced, and data are sought. In monitoring, however, the process may also call for inductive logic. The program manager is confronted with facts and observations. These may be not only unanticipated but also unwanted, but they must be interpreted and their meaning in the program context must be assessed.

The Evaluation Process

If evaluation is defined as comparing something to something else with a view to making a decision, then the elements of the evaluation process are given in its definition: There is the thing itself, the standard against which it is to be evaluated, the act of comparison or judgment, and the decision itself (see Figure 3).

Nevertheless, this model is inadequate on several counts. We must be concerned with the basis on which standards are established, determining which data are important, comparison, and transforming comparison into judgment. A more elaborate model may be needed (see Figure 4).

To begin with, we should recognize that we seldom make direct comparisons between outcomes and standards; what we compare are data about outcomes or other relevant phenomena. Data are not achieved without effort. They result from the application of instruments of various sorts. But which measures are to be used? The answer depends partly on what is to be mea-

Figure 3. Schematic of Decision-Making Components

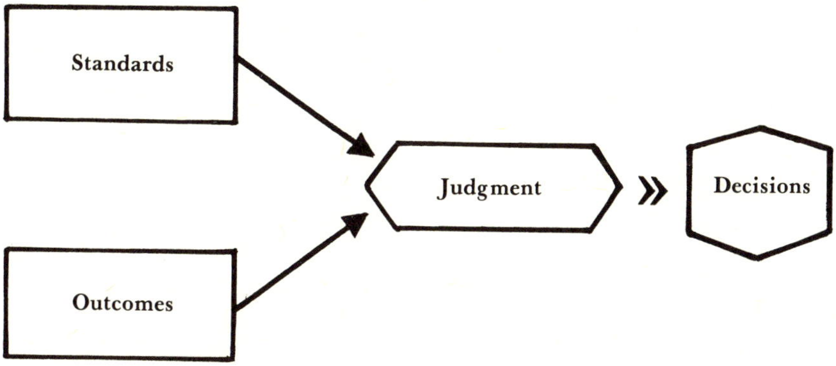

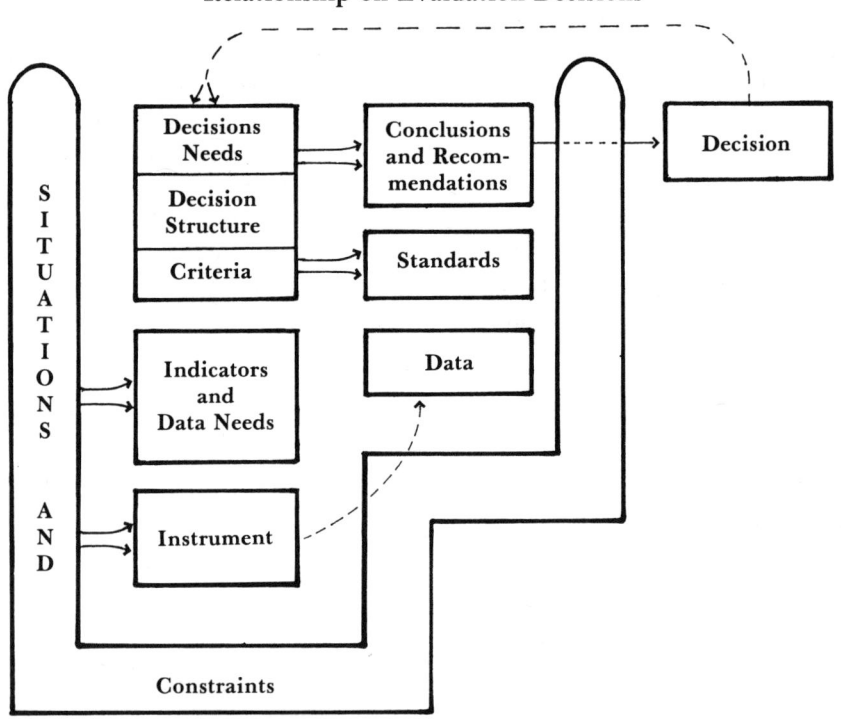

Figure 4. Schematic of Situations and Constraints Relationship on Evaluation Decisions

sured—on the evalutive criteria and the indicators we will use to represent them—and partly on the situation in which measurement will occur. In other words, evaluators use whichever measures will yield the data needed for decisions within the limits that must be observed. The same considerations also affect the selection of standards, that is, the degree to which criteria are to be met.

Effective evaluation depends largely on the choice of appropriate evaluative criteria, since they provide the basis for choosing both measures and standards of comparison. It is commonly assumed that evaluation criteria are simply refinements of program intents or objectives. This assumption is true when decisions are based on whether or not intended outcomes have been achieved. Some decisions, however, may call for other kinds of information; the decision to adopt a course of action, for example, may call for determining whether certain assumed preconditions actually exist. Standards, as understood here, represent quantification of criteria and are derived from them. Levels of expectation may be conditioned by objectives (if objectives are involved), by situational or other constraints, or by previous experience, or even by what is being evaluated. Adjustments of expectations in the light of experience are quite common and are not always indefensible.

It is also apparent that indicators used to represent criteria will depend on situational factors. The time at which an evaluation must be performed, the accessibility of various kinds of data, and the conditions under which evaluation is done all enter into the choice. Thus, we see that evaluative criteria may or may not derive from program intents, but that they still definitely depend on anticipated decisions. In fact, to be used as a basis for decision, an evaluation must address the criteria accepted by the decision maker.

Decisions are made by people who use criteria according to rules, although neither criteria nor rules are always spelled out or unanimously accepted. If evaluations are to serve decision-making purposes usefully, the criteria used in the evaluation and those used in the decision must be compatible. For evaluators, this means identifying decision makers, the criteria they will accept, and the rules under which decisions will be made. If there are disagreements about criteria, either these must be resolved or all criteria must be served to make a variety of judgments possible from the same evaluation.

In some "wrap-up" evaluations, the intent is to serve a number of decisions and decision makers. Because it is difficult to predict either all the kinds of decisions that will be attempted on the basis of such an evaluation or all their criteria, multiple-decision evaluations often appear to be summative and to concentrate on how well an effort succeeded on its own terms or in terms of some set of arbitrarily chosen external criteria. To be useful, their decision applicability must be understood clearly, and the decisions they are to serve must be researched as thoroughly as in single-decision evaluations.

The model presented here identifies the elements involved in program evaluation and illustrates their relationships in terms of derivations. In this sense, it is a description of program evaluation as a process. The CIPP model of Stufflebeam (1971) and the Countenance model of Stake (1967) — to use two widely known examples — do quite different things. The CIPP model shows the relationship of evaluation to various aspects of program decision making and proposes four varieties of evaluation corresponding to types of decision needs. The Countenance model can more aptly be described as a catalogue of the information needed for a multiple-decision or wrap-up evaluation. It neither describes the process nor shows its relationship to programming needs.

Participation in Evaluation

Cooperative extension programs are characterized by a high level of clientele involvement in their design and execution. Since clients are participating actively in making program decisions, they are also a part of the evaluation picture. Obviously, they can be of immense help in data collection, but this function is probably their least important form of participation. Just as they contribute to decisions about program directions, clients can also help determine how the accomplishment of these objectives will be measured and judged.

In addition, some local people both inside and outside the extension system are already making authoritative evaluations of extension programs and basing actions on these evaluations. The criteria used by local legislators in making budget decisions, for example, are of crucial importance. Evaluations addressed to those decision makers are not likely to be effective unless the operative criteria are known and addressed.

Monitoring

Cooperative extension programs are adaptable: Not only are programs developed in response to specific local situations and needs, they also tend to be flexible. Individual extension professionals, paraprofessionals, and volunteer leaders all work independently and with considerable authority to adjust programs to fit circumstances. Personnel become independent and continuous evaluators. Program quality—its fit and the demands of the situation—depends on the quality of this monitoring activity.

Although it is probably impossible to plan monitoring in detail, several key steps can be taken to improve the quality of monitoring:

1. The program objectives should be thoroughly familiar to all staff members and volunteers. Criteria for success or failure should be defined. Tentative scenarios should be developed, indicating what should or should not be happening at various stages of the program.

2. Key decision points in the program should be identified. Contingency plans can be made to identify who will initiate the decision process and on what evidence, who will take part in it and how, and the kinds of criteria to be applied.

3. A set of monitoring procedures appropriate to the circumstances should be established to allow for consultation and information sharing at critical points.

4. Particular attention should be given to identifying potential catastrophes—things calling for emergency action. Signs for early recognition, procedures for acknowledging them, and immediate responses should be known in detail by everyone involved. Longer-run procedures for resolving such situations should also be devised.

EMIS

The Extension Management Information System (EMIS) can be an important evaluation resource, but it is not an evaluation system in itself and will not even promote program evaluation unless made to do so. As a reporting system, EMIS is severely limited, in that it measures only inputs. Such measures are directly useful in the monitoring of educational opportunity and use of staff resources, but EMIS simply does not report accomplishments. Outcomes enter the picture at the planning stage. Individual plans of work and the reporting of line-items that represent them reflect program objectives. The reports are coded so that the effort reported can be allocated to objectives both at state and local levels.

Improving the usefulness of EMIS for evaluation, then, begins with improving the quality of the plan—making sure that the objectives are good ones and that criteria exist for recognizing when plans are being realized. These objectives and their associated criteria should be the basis for assessing achievement and planning the next program cycle.

The need for uniformity, both at national and state levels and from year to year, makes it difficult to adjust actual reported data, but this possibility should be under constant study. Constantly improving reporting methods will make accurate reporting easier.

Finally, program decision makers at all levels should use EMIS. To do so, however, demands a clear analysis of problems. With a decision need identified and criteria selected, planners can go to EMIS for help.

Conclusions

In conclusion, the example of the cooperative extension service has illustrated how program evaluation can be used to increase the impact of continuing education activities on performances. The following guidelines are offered:
1. Encourage people associated with the program to focus on desired results.
2. Use load involvement in program development to increase commitment to results.
3. Apply evaluation procedures and findings to strengthen the setting of objectives.
4. Increase commitment to the use of evaluation findings by encouraging participation in planning and by conducting evaluation activities.
5. Monitor program processes and outcomes by means of evaluation.
6. Make evaluation relate directly to decision making.
7. Follow sound evaluation planning and implementation procedures.

Additional Resources

Evaluation (General)

Guba, E., and Lincoln, Y. S. *Effective Evaluation.* San Francisco: Jossey-Bass, 1981.

Popham, W. J. *Educational Evaluation.* Englewood Cliffs, N.J.: Prentice-Hall, 1975.

Rossi, P. H., and Williams, W. *Evaluation of Social Programs.* New York: Seminar Press, 1972.

Evaluation in Extension

Bennett, C. *Analyzing Impacts of Extension Programs.* Washington, D.C.: United States Department of Agriculture Extension Service, 1977.

Bruce, R. L. *Programming for Intangibles.* Information Bulletin 179. Ithaca, N.Y.: Cornell University, 1981.

Byrn, D. (Ed.). *Evaluation in Extension.* Topeka, Kans.: H. M. Ives, 1959.

Cosby, A. G., and Wetherill, G. R. *Resources in Evaluation of Rural Development.* Mississippi State: Southern Rural Development Center, Mississippi State University, 1977.

Gross, J. *Cooperative Extension Evaluation Planner.* Washington, D.C.: United States Department of Agriculture Extension Service, 1976.

Miller, R. W. *Evaluation Research in Rural Development: Concepts, Methods, Issues.* Ithaca, N.Y.: Northeast Regional Center for Rural Development, Cornell University, 1979.

Steele, S. M., and Black, R. *Evaluation of the Attainment of Objectives in Adult Education.* Syracuse, N.Y.: Syracuse University, 1973.

Data Collection and Instrument Design

Berdie, D. R. *Questionnaires: Design and Use.* Metuchen, N.J.: Scarecrow Press, 1974.

Bradburn, N., and others. *Improving Interview Method and Questionnaire Design.* San Francisco: Jossey-Bass, 1979.

Bruce, R. L., and Puerta, I. *Data Collection and Low-Income Audiences.* Ithaca, N.Y.: Department of Education, Cornell University, 1972.

Fiedler, J. *Field Research: A Manual.* San Francisco: Jossey-Bass, 1978.

Payne, S. L. *The Art of Asking Questions.* Princeton, N.J.: Princeton University Press, 1951.

Sudman, S. *Applied Sampling.* New York: Academic Press, 1976.

Warwick, D. P. *The Sample Survey: Theory and Practice.* New York: McGraw-Hill, 1975.

References

Stake, R. "The Countenance of Educational Evaluation." *Teachers College Record,* 1967, *68* (7), 106–128.

Stufflebeam, D., and others. *Educational Evaluation and Decision Making.* Bloomington, Ind.: Phi Delta Kappa, 1971.

United States Department of Agriculture. *1981–1982 Directory of Professional Workers in State Agricultural Experiment Stations and Other Cooperating State Institutions.* Agricultural Handbook No. 305. (Rev. ed.) Washington, D.C.: U.S. Government Printing Office, 1982.

Robert L. Bruce is professor of extension and continuing education at Cornell University. He is spending this year at the University of Agriculture in Malaysia as a Fulbright–Hayes Scholar.

Problem-oriented education is used to ensure correspondence between professional performance and professional criteria that have educational implications.

Strengthening the Relationship Between Professional Education and Performance

Joseph S. Gonnella
Carter Zeleznik

This chapter describes an approach to continuing professional education designed to improve performance. The approach is general and applicable to various professional fields. It permits continuing education to be related to the practical aspects of professional behavior, since it is based on the scientific problem-solving method. It also takes individual and group needs and values into account. Continuing professional education is justified to the extent that it helps professionals perform more effectively. It is problem-oriented because professionals should identify and attempt to solve problems in their respective fields (Cross, 1969; Escovitz, 1973; Weed, 1970).

Problems, of course, come in many shapes and sizes. Consequently, one underlying principle is that, before attempting to solve a problem, we should determine that the problem is real and that we understand its dimensions. In the language of medicine, this process could be described as diagnosis before therapy (Brown, 1969; Miller, 1967). Unfortunately, this underlying principle is frequently honored only in the breach.

Professional education and performance are very complex topics, and we must be very cautious in working with what is obvious but also complex. If a physician is a cardiologist, for example, he or she is likely to be competent in treating heart disease, but may still need to learn about infectious disease, for the small percentage of heart patients who develop infections. In any case, this physician's educational needs should be determined empirically. We shall examine both professional performance and education in some detail while attempting to integrate these two topics.

Professional Performance

Educators are often tempted to assume that substandard professional performance is caused by inadequate knowledge, skills, or attitudes on the part of the professional involved (White, 1980). There are, however, many other influences on performance that we should consider before attempting educational solutions to performance deficiencies. For example if a pilot makes a poor landing, a physician fails to explain the potential complications of a drug to a patient, a teacher does not collect baseline data on students, or a lawyer initiates a legal action on inadequate grounds, there may be many reasons for these inadequate performances, and only some of the causes may be addressed appropriately by education. The pilot's failure to land the airplane correctly may have been the result of alcoholism or medication or of unreported weather conditions. The physician's workload on a given day may have been excessive, leaving little time for consultation with patients. Administrative considerations may interfere with teachers' collecting pretest information about students, or the students may object to having the data collected.

When the various possible causal factors for inadequate performance have been examined, attention has to be given to how severe the deficiency is and to priorities for the relative importance of the problems and their susceptibility to various kinds of educational interventions (Fleisher, 1973; Youel, 1975; Osborne, 1982). Only then can meaningful decisions be made about educational interventions. Whether the actual causes of inadequate performance have been identified, and whether the educational program selected to correct it has been appropriate, can often be decided only on the basis of both short- and long-term follow-up observations, but these are rarely conducted.

Thus, professionals are confronted with real problems rooted in many factors, only some of which will yield to education. Likewise, educators are frequently trapped into providing solutions for problems over which they may have only limited control, and which they may not understand.

Criteria for Ideal Performance

We must start our definition of criteria by defining professional goals and objectives that are scientifically or practically sound, socially justified, and achievable. We can represent our statement of ideal performance in terms of a formal set of criteria, with the understanding that only some of these performance criteria will have educational implications (see Figure 1).

These criteria are derived from books, articles, lectures, and other scientific or professional communications based on countless observations and measurements. Obviously, there will be room for confusion and disagreement about specific criteria or standards and their application under particular circumstances. Nevertheless, in evaluating performance in any professional field, we do look for correspondence between the given professional criteria and the performance of a given professional.

As the goal of professional research is to validate professional criteria, so the goal of continuing professional education is to ensure the possibility of reasonable correspondence between those professional criteria that have educational implications, on the one hand, and professional performance, on the other. Too often, however, continuing professional education consists only of individuals stating their impressions of professional criteria, without finding out either the extent to which criteria and performance already correspond or why this is not the case.

The goal of continuing professional education, as described above is to ensure the development of proficiencies that can be translated into professional performance. Properly speaking, then, education is connected not to performance but to proficiency.

The Relationship Between Proficiency and Performance

One common illness that may be the subject of programs in continuing medical education is chronic obstructive pulmonary disease (COPD), usually associated with a history of smoking cigarettes. Multiple physiological changes occur as the result of smoking. Eventually, the individual is able to breathe only with difficulty. Among other things, treatment for this condition clearly consists of getting afflicted individuals to discontinue smoking. Programs in continuing medical education may be devoted to descriptions of the physiological changes, to discussions of laboratory procedures that may be used, and to a review of advanced techniques for treating late-stage COPD. What may be needed is information about how to get patients to stop smoking. This need, however, may interfere with a physician's own smoking habits or with the economy of a particular geographical area (for example, many people in a given region may grow tobacco or manufacture cigarettes). Moreover, the success rate of such treatment is likely to be very low, since there may be little incentive for physicians to help patients give up smoking. Health insurers may be willing to pay for pulmonary function tests, but not for time spent in patient education. Thus, physicians may have the requisite knowledge about a prob-

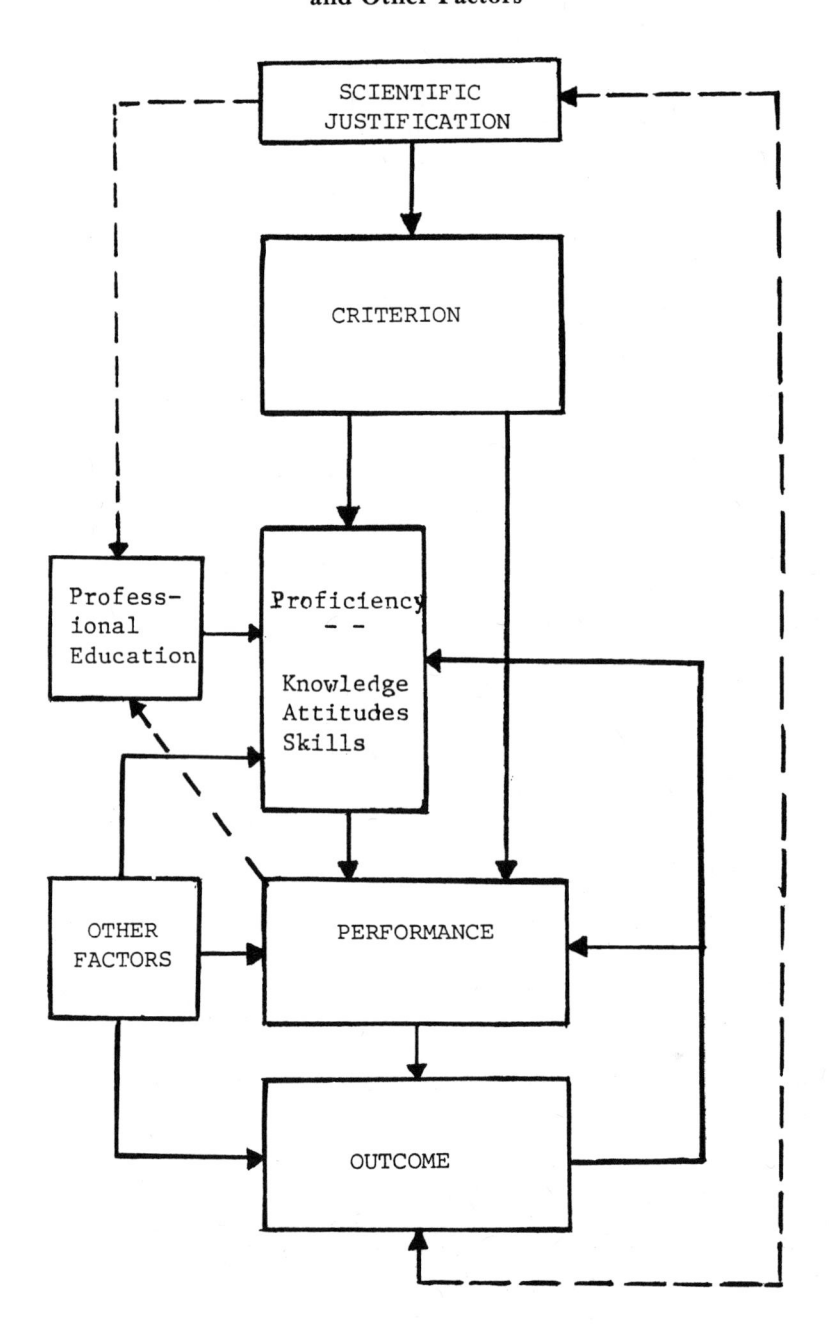

Figure 1. Flowchart Illustrating Relationships Among Proficiency, Performance, Outcomes, Criteria, Professional Education, and Other Factors

lem, but lack the skills and attitudes needed to manage the problem. It is likely that educational programs on COPD will be devoted to the cognitive issues involved, but will gloss over other issues. Adequate professional criteria with regard to helping patients stop smoking may not even exist, much less have educational implications.

Thus, continuing professional education may be conducted with varying degrees of appropriateness. Some professionals may need no additional education; others may be partially proficient or competent, needing instruction only in certain skills or attitudes; still others may lack both essential knowledge and necessary skills and attitudes.

Diagnosis of Performance Deficiencies

Careful diagnosis is always needed for ascertaining not only the deficiencies involved in substandard performance but also the extent to which education can remedy them. For example, in medicine, the multiple roles a physician is expected to play can affect his or her performance. Physicians are obviously clinicians and must make various diagnostic and therapeutic judgments. Thus, they must be able to collect information and need to have some skill in taking histories, performing physical examinations, and ordering laboratory tests. To obtain this information, however, physicians must be able to communicate with patients and others. They must be able to function as managers of various kinds of resources. They must also be able to interact with patients' families and even with their communities. Thus, they must be able to function as educators. A physician may be competent or proficient in some areas but lacking in others, even while working with the same patient. Therefore, educational diagnosis should assess specific proficiencies and specific deficiencies and then ascertain their relationship to an identified performance problem.

Situational factors may also affect professional performance, either directly or through interaction with various other aspects of the physician's proficiency (Gonnella and Storey, 1981; Lessinger, 1973). The expectations of the patient may also play a role in how a physician performs. Similarly, physicians are likely to perform in a manner they perceive to be like that of their professional colleagues within a specialty area, a community, or an institution. Indeed, physicians' performance may vary, depending on whether they are working in clinics or in offices (Lewis, 1973). If there are conflicting responsibilities, if many patients require attention, or if a physician is tired and it is the end of the day, then performance may be expected to suffer. Obviously, physicians are affected by medicine's reward system, including such factors as professional recognition by colleagues, financial reimbursement, and third-party payers' rules and regulations. If either a rich assortment of technical resources or skilled specialists are available, then the pattern of performance may vary accordingly. Age and other factors relating to personal characteristics also come into play in quite complex ways (Clute, 1963; Joint Commission on the Accreditation of Hospitals, 1974; Peterson and others, 1956; Richards and Cohen, 1981).

In diagnosing deficiencies amenable to education, special attention should be directed to examining environmental factors, as well as those related to professional competence. Thus, in medicine, various patient factors are of great importance (Gonnella and Zeleznik, 1974). These include the patient's willingness and ability to comply with medical regimens and to communicate promptly and accurately about changes resulting from treatment. In this regard, the role of the family may be crucial. Other social factors and general environmental factors may also come into play. For example, a physician may advise a COPD patient not to smoke, but the hospital in which the patient is receiving care may have a cigarette machine in the lobby. The patient may also simply be unwilling to discontinue smoking or may get little or no support from family members; in fact, smoking may be expected in the individual's social environment.

When single deficiencies can be identified and traced to specific performance factors, problems can be corrected through educational programs, but when multiple deficiencies have roots in cognitive, affective, and psychomotor factors, the effectiveness of educational programs becomes questionable (Corcoran, 1979; Lewis and Hassanein, 1970; Richards and Cohen, 1981). Even when some aspects of a problem have obvious educational implications, it may be preferable to concentrate on environmental factors whose impact on performance may be greater than the impact of simple deficiencies. This is particularly true when opportunities exist to make changes in the reward system or when it is possible to introduce new role models for professionals to emulate.

Objective diagnosis techniques are best in continuing professional education, even though they may be expensive and may be perceived as intrusive. Multiple hypotheses should be considered and data collected to support or refute the most probable hypothesis. A variety of diagnostic techniques can be considered, including professional audits, examinations, and direct observations of actual professional performance. A professional can also be asked what he perceives his deficiencies to be. Unfortunately, perceived needs are not likely to correspond closely to actual needs, as identified through other means (AMA, 1966; Duff and Cheung, 1979; Youel, 1975).

Just as physicians are well advised not to treat mere symptoms, so should educators avoid presenting educational programs merely because some performance deficiency has been observed, nor should participants enroll in continuing education just because courses are conveniently available. In making an educational diagnosis, as in making a medical diagnosis, the underlying causes of a deficiency should be investigated. In most cases, investigators should expect to find multifaceted problems only partially subject to correction through education (Coordinating Council on Medical Education, 1979; Gonnella and Storey, 1981; Griner, 1977; McAuliff, 1978; Manning, 1978; U.S. Department of Health, Education, and Welfare, 1977). Nevertheless, investigators should consider the role of various components of professional proficiency and competence, as well as environmental factors affecting both proficiency and performance.

Specific Evaluation of How Proficiency Affects Peformance

Educational diagnosis may suggest that inadequate performance results from deficiencies that are amenable to educational intervention. Of course, it is relatively easy to find out whether or not an individual has the requisite knowledge to perform at a certain professional level. There are multiple indications, however, that performance deficiencies do not result from simple ignorance; moreover, vital information can be obtained through reading or from other persons—there is a big difference between not knowing something and knowing that one does not know it.

The various components of proficiency can be studied both separately and in combination. Knowledge is probably the easiest component to study, but only with the caveats suggested above. Written and other forms of examinations can also be used to measure knowledge of essential information. Simple ignorance may not point to specifically educational solutions, and it is also true than evidence of knowledge suggests that simply imparting facts is likely to be a misdirected remedial effort.

Data-gathering skill, as another aspect of clinical competence, can be evaluated through observation, practical examinations, simulations, and similar techniques. Again, deficient data-gathering skills may reflect personality problems or forms of task interference that may not be subject to correction through education. Clinical judgment may be tested orally, in various kinds of simulations, or by reviewing the professional's written records of case material. Although this approach most obviously applies to the medical profession, other professions may benefit from analogous application of its principles.

Professional attitudes, interests, and habits can be assessed through observation, oral examination, self-report, peer evaluation, the use of consultants, calling upon patients or clients, and review of appropriate records.

While it may be difficult to define precisely what ideal professional performance should be in a given situation, it may be even more difficult to specify which proficiency is required for desired performance outcomes. An individual may accomplish the same task through a variety of different approaches; similarly, it may be difficult to measure proficiencies in various areas as well as measuring performance in many instances (Botticelli and Anderson, 1981; Goran, Williamson, and Gonnella, 1973; Levine and McGuire, 1970; McCarthy and Gonnella, 1967; Payne, 1978). Thus, educators have to tolerate uncertainty in the planning, implementation, and evaluation of their programs and should recognize their limitations in achieving desired performance outcomes.

Relating Program Structure to Learners' Needs

Our discussion so far has focused on assessing the need for a program relative to its content. Of course, we must also be concerned about educational procedure itself. How much attention should be paid to questions of format, environment, and technology? To what extent should continuing education be practical and take place in the work setting? To what extent should it take place in conference rooms at resort hotels? How much attention should be given to individual learning differences and preferences? Certainly, if a surgeon is having difficulty because of inadequate manual skills, lectures on dexterity are likely to be ineffective. Nevertheless, most continuing professional education still consists of information transfer, based on the assumption that the main deficiencies of learners are cognitive.

To a very significant extent, a careful needs assessment can determine the form an educational program should take. Acquisition or improvement of various psychomotor skills, for example, requires opportunities for practicing them. Many effective approaches to knowledge deficiencies are possible: Some individuals may profit from reading books and journals; others, from attending lectures. Still others may respond to audiovisual technology. In these areas, individual preferences can easily be accommodated. The affective domain is probably the most difficult area for continuing medical education, even though inappropriate attitudes may represent the greatest source of professional incompetence and poor performance. In general, educators have been reluctant to confront attitudinal problems in learners, both out of respect for learners' personality differences and because of attitudes' relative imperviousness to education (Costello, 1977).

Changing attitudes through education requires great skill. It is true that peer pressure and role-model behavior may have transient effects on some individuals, but considerable empirical investigation will be required before any firm guidelines, except for what not to do, can be offered in this area. Lectures and other kinds of passivity-inducing programs are unlikely to engender meaningful attitudinal changes, nor are confrontational techniques likely to be useful. The most important principle is probably to maintain awareness that attitudinal factors may be involved in any educational program and at all stages of program development, from needs assessment through long-term follow-up.

Diagnostic Question Checklist for Continuing Professional Education

As a summary and a means of making the above discussion more useful to the reader, the following checklist of questions is proposed.

A. Professional Performance Standards
   1. To what extent do criteria supported by scientific studies describe standards of ideal professional performance?
   2. To what extent do learners already agree with these criteria?
B. Actual Professional Performance
   1. To what extent did performance conform to ideal criteria prior to the proposed program? What additional information would provide a more adequate determination?
   2. How much variation in actual performance exists among prospective learners?
   3. To what extent are learners aware of their own performance deficiencies?
C. Analysis of Performance Deficiencies
   1. When performance does not conform to ideal criteria, to what extent is this inadequacy a function of learner competence? To what extent is it a function of other factors? How is the cause assessed? How accurate are the assessments?
   2. When factors other than learner proficiency are involved, what attention will be given to correcting them?
   3. When performance problems can be traced to deficiencies, which proficiency components are responsible? How is this responsibility assessed? How adequately?
D. Attribution of Deficiencies to Educationally Remediable Factors
   1. Prior to the program, what evidence exists that proficiency shortcomings accounting for performance deficiencies are remediable through education?
   2. What evidence exists in this regard after the program has been conducted?
E. Incorporating Learning Preferences and Learning Styles
   1. What special preferences or needs do individual learners have with regard to how information should be presented to increase proficiency? What is the evidence?
   2. To what extent are group educational programs justified or necessary as means of correcting deficiencies? What is the evidence?

The Likelihood of Continuing Professional Education's Becoming Performance-Oriented

Relatively few of the foregoing ideas are original: The literature on continuing education has already discussed these matters extensively. There remains, however, a need to translate theory into practice, something that does not come about easily or quickly. Various efforts in this direction have been made; perhaps the most noteworthy of these has been the Continuing Education Systems Project, funded by the Veterans Administration and conducted jointly with the American Association of Medical Colleges (Corcoran, 1979; Suter, 1981). This project has been concerned with introducing a system of accreditation into continuing medical and health-professional education, using a series of 137 elements. Among these elements are recommendations for conducting and evaluating needs assessments; establishing performance criteria; and identifying potential problems and concerns by using current learning technologies, self-directed learning skills, aggregate descriptive data from multiple sources, and involvement of learners (Suter, 1981).

Nevertheless, there have been two major problems associated with this project. One involves using these elements for accreditation, and the other involves obtaining compliance with the accreditation system from those who produce or use continuing education programs. For one thing, the demand for improved continuing education has come largely from the top down: Users of these programs want to believe in their ability to determine their own needs through introspection, and that they are mature and independent individuals; they fear that external needs assessment would be invasive and nonproductive. For another, continuing education providers are eager to avoid making potential participants uncomfortable and so are reluctant to ask too many questions or make too many observations about learners' professional competence of performance.

Guidelines for continuing education will very likely continue to be general, and the connections between performance and continuing education are likely to remain loose. For change to occur, there must be an effective demand for change. Such demand may be economic: If significant technological changes are occurring in a given profession and making old knowledge obsolete, individuals working in the field will seek to learn the skills and knowledge needed to accommodate the technological changes. Obviously, however, we cannot predicate changes such as those suggested in this chapter solely on the basis of such technological advances. Thus far, neither producers nor users of continuing education have generated any demand for the kind of approach we have suggested here and that is already implicit in the Continuing Education Systems Project.

We believe that continuing education should be largely (if not entirely) in the service of quality control within a given field: If quality is already optimal, then there is no need for change and no need for continuing education. Quality control must be a continuous process involving constant reassessment of individuals by themselves or by others. In certain areas, all professionals have continuing education needs. Given significant quality-assurance problems in all quarters of contemporary society, we need change and, thus, continuing professional education. We lack that commitment to quality-control procedures through which the need for change can be recognized and the relationship between performance and continuing education can be strengthened. Some steps in this direction have been taken; in medicine, for example, professional-standards review organizations (PSROs) have been established in the United States, presumably to ensure the quality of professional health care. There is little evidence, however, that PSROs have made any kind of contribution to developing continuing medical education programs along the lines suggested (U.S. Department of Health, Education, and Welfare, 1974). The malpractice crisis affecting many professions can also be seen as a kind of quality-control mechanism. Again, though, there is little evidence that this crisis has encouraged the use of continuing education as a solution to proficiency and performance problems. Indeed, such data that do exist strongly suggest that performance deficiencies are infrequently due to the kinds of cognitive deficiencies that can be corrected through traditional continuing education.

One practical proposal for the medical field would be for insurance carriers to monitor the quality of care given by those individuals whom they insure against malpractice and to encourage them to participate in appropriate quality-assurance programs, only one aspect of which would involve continuing education based on observed deficiencies. These provisions could be either conditions for continued coverage or incentives to lower premiums. (But are such lower premiums possible, even with optimal continuing education? To our knowledge, no cost-benefit studies have ever been conducted to answer this question.) Employers of professionals in other fields could also attempt to establish programs relating continuing education to quality control.

Incentives to quality are likely to have long-term benefits and payoffs, and if the payoff to an insurance company is deferred for five or ten years, this proposal may seem unattractive. Increasingly, therefore, existing continuing education is concerned with short-term considerations, most of which have little to offer either to society or to the search for improved quality in the professions.

Instead of massive conversion of our educational efforts, what we probably need is documentation of the cost-benefit advantages related to selected performance-oriented continuing professional educational programs. If change is to occur and be meaningful, scientific experimentation should provide its basis.

It is important to emphasize that the ideas presented here are primarily concerned with formal continuing education as it relates to professional performance. When individuals undertake continuing education on the basis of their own interests and without seeking specific professional recognition for doing so, they should not be constrained by criteria of need, as described above. Even in these cases, however, some effort should be made to ensure that the program has still enhanced proficiency.

In summary, then, for formal (required) continuing professional education programs to affect performance, existing performance must be examined and overall deficiencies identified. These should be analyzed so that priorities can be set with regard to which deficiencies should be corrected first and which are likely to be corrected through educational intervention. In general, only if proficiency is lacking is education likely to be an effective solution. It should be recognized that the most frequent deficiencies are associated with attitudes and with environmental factors that prevent or discourage optimal professional performance. Although we may learn a great deal from general analyses of professional behavior, in most cases individualized educational diagnoses are in order. The active involvement of learners in their own education (which necessarily includes diagnosis of educational needs, as distinct from other needs) is essential. The educational literature should also devote increasing attention to reporting on programs that have used the scientific methods described in this chapter.

References

American Medical Association (AMA). *A Description of the Physician's Inventory of His Own Continuing Medical Education.* Washington, D.C.: American Medical Association, 1966.

Botticelli, M., and Anderson, A. "M.D.-Level Competence in Internal Medicine, Objectives, and Flexible Clerkship." *Archives of Internal Medicine,* 1981, *141,* 235.

Brown, C. R., Jr. "Patient Care and Continuing Medical Education: Diagnosis Before Therapy." Paper presented at the Association of American Medical Colleges annual meeting, 1969.

Clute, K. F. *The General Practitioner.* Toronto: University of Toronto Press, 1963.

Coordinating Council on Medical Education. *The Continuing Competence of Physicians.* Chicago, Ill.: Coordinating Council on Medical Education, 1973.

Corcoran, P. "Keynote Address, Seventh Annual Conference on Continuing Medical Education." *Continuing Medical Education Newsletter,* 1979, *8,* 3.

Costello, G. "Continuing Medical Education—Past, Present, and Potential for the Future." *Journal of the South Carolina Medical Society,* November 1977, 488-490.

Cross, H. "Educational Needs as Determined by the Problem-Oriented Medical Record." Paper presented at the Association of American Medical Colleges meeting, 1969.

Duff, W., and Cheung, M. "CME Program Evaluation: Long-Term Retention." *Continuing Medical Education Newsletter,* 1979, *8* (13), 7-9.

Escovitz, G. "The Continuing Education of Physicians—Its Relationship to Quality of Care Evaluation." *Medical Clinics of North America,* 1973, *57* (4), 1135-1147.
Fleisher, D. "Priorities and Data Bases: Their Relationship to Continuing Education." In A. N. Charters and R. J. Blakely (Eds.), *Fostering the Growing Need to Learn.* Washington, D.C.: U.S. Department of Health, Education, and Welfare, 1973.
Gonnella, J., and Storey, P. "Continuing Medical Education and Clinical Competence: A Matrix Approach to a Complex Problem." *Continuing Medical Education Newsletter,* 1981, *10* (4), 3-15.
Goran, M., Williamson, J., and Gonnella, J. "The Validity of Patient Management Problems." *Journal of Medical Education,* 1973, *48* (2), 171-177.
Griner, P. "Evaluation and Continuing Education of the General Internist." *Archives of Internal Medicine,* 1977, *137,* 1319-1320.
Joint Commission on the Accreditation of Hospitals. *Annotated Bibliography on References on the Interface Between Peer Review Findings and Continuing Health Professions Education.* Washington, D.C.: Joint Commission on the Accreditation of Hospitals, 1974.
Lessinger, L. "Effective Caring: An Approach to a Rational Scheme for Financing Continuing Education for Health Manpower." In A. N. Charters and R. J. Blakely (Eds.), *Fostering the Growing Need to Learn.* Washington, D.C.: U.S. Department of Health, Education, and Welfare, 1973.
Levine, H., and McGuire, C. "The Validity of Multiple-Choice Achievement Tests and Measures of Competence in Medicine." *American Educational Research Journal,* 1970, *7* (1), 69.
Lewis, A. "The Use of Analytical Techniques to Determine Health Manpower Requirements for Educational Planning—or, How Do I Find Out What Skills and Knowledges to Teach?" In A. N. Charters and R. J. Blakely (Eds.), *Fostering the Growing Need to Learn.* Washington, D.C.: U.S. Department of Health, Education, and Welfare, 1973.
Lewis, C., and Hassanein, R. "Continuing Medical Education—an Epidemiological Evaluation." *New England Journal of Medicine,* 1970, *282* (5), 254-259.
McAuliff, W. "Studies of Process-Outcome Correlations in Medical Care Evaluations: A Critique." *Medical Care,* 1978, *16* (11), 907.
McCarthy, W., and Gonnella, J. "The Simulated Patient Management Problem: A Technique for Evaluating and Teaching Clinical Competence." *British Journal of Medical Education,* 1967, *1* (5), 348-352.
Miller, G. E. "Continuing Education for What?" *Journal of Medical Education,* 1967, *42,* 320.
Osborne, C. "Assessing Needs for Community Hospital Continuing Medical Education." *Medical Care,* 1982, *20* (9), 967-971.
Payne, B. "The Medical Record as a Basis for Assessing Physician Competence." Unpublished paper, 1978.
Peterson, O., and others. "An Analytic Study of North Carolina General Practice: 1953-1954." *Journal of Medical Education,* 1956, *31* (1), part 2.
Richards, R., and Cohen, R. *The Value and Limitations of Physician Participation in Traditional Forms of Continuing Medical Education.* Kalamazoo, Mich.: Educational Services, The Upjohn Company, 1981.
Suter, E. "Continuing Education of Health Professionals: Proposal for a Definition of Quality." *Journal of Medical Education,* 1981, *56* (8), 687-707.
U.S. Department of Health, Education, and Welfare. *PSRO: An Educational Force for Improving Quality of Care.* Washington, D.C.: Bureau of Quality Assurance, U.S. Department of Health, Education, and Welfare, 1974.
U.S. Department of Health, Education, and Welfare. *Competence in the Medical Professions: A Strategy.* Washington, D.C.: U.S. Department of Health, Education, and Welfare, 1977.

Weed, L. *Medical Records, Medical Education, and Patient Care.* Chicago: Year Book Medical Publishers, 1970.

White, C. W., and others. "Efficacy of Traditional Continuing Medical Education in Changing Physician Knowledge and Behavior in the Care of Patients with Acute Myocardial Infarction." Paper presented at the Association of American Colleges annual meeting, 1980.

Youel, D. B. *Profiles of Problems: Setting Priorities for Our Time and Energy.* Kalamazoo, Mich.: Southwestern Michigan Area Health Education Center, 1975.

Joseph S. Gonnella, M.D., is professor of medicine, associate dean, and director of the Office of Medical Education at Jefferson Medical College, Philadelphia. Upon completion of medical school and his residency, he undertook a year of study with George E. Miller at the University of Illinois, College of Medicine, as a fellow in medical education. He has published numerous articles pertaining to medical education and patient care.

Carter Zeleznik is research assistant professor of psychiatry and associate director of the Office of Medical Education at Jefferson Medical College, Philadelphia. He has participated in various programs related to patient-care evaluation and has been a consultant to numerous organizations interested in this topic, including both the Joint Commission on the Accreditation of Hospitals and the Continuing Education Systems Project, sponsored by the Veterans Administration.

Becoming an adult educator is not achieved by acquiring facility in professing on subjects.

A Perspective on Preparing Adult Educators

G. L. Carter

We prepare people to function professionally as adult educators in order to enable them to perform more adequately in practice. Functioning as a practitioner involves substantially more than being exposed to the subject of adult education. Yet, the institutions in which adult educators are prepared are oriented principally toward preparing students to profess on the subjects they study. This occurs mainly because their instructors profess on their subjects or fields of study. The reward system of the university sanctions professors' efforts to extend the subjects on which they profess, rather than to improve students' abilities to function as practitioners.

What is critically needed for adult education practitioners is preparation than enables them to function in such a manner that their efforts make a recognizable impact on those whom they teach.

This chapter presents a perspective for developing more adequate programs of study. The following points are included: (1) the nature of graduate study in adult education; (2) demands made on practitioners and how knowledge can be drawn upon; and (3) most pressing needs.

This chapter goes beyond Clark's (1980) analysis of writings about adult development and the experience of graduate education. It puts forth views of what should be considered.

Graduate Study in Adult Education

Who are the students who major in adult education? What is adult education practice like? What could help us understand the nature of a process that might provide adequate preparation for practitioners? I am confining this discussion to those who plan to be practitioners—those concerned with matters as they occur in their natural settings.

Characteristics of Students. The stated purposes of several hundred adults who have applied as graduate students in adult education reflect three kinds of applicants:
1. Those who want to learn things that will enhance their abilities to function as adult educators.
2. Those whose present employment or anticipated employment requires that they have a graduate degree. In some instances it is thought (or specified) that such a degree should be in adult education. In other cases the requirement is simply that of an appropriate degree,
3. Those whose principal concern is acquiring a credential that is expected to enable them to compete more successfully for positions or promotions.

It is likely that two or more of these three purposes exist for most who seek to study adult education. However, in many cases one of these purposes is dominant. Experience in working with students entering with such differing purposes reveals that the dominant purpose makes a difference in the way students approach their studies. Prior academic preparation of those entering graduate study may also help explain their expectations.

To obtain an idea of the prior academic preparation of those studying adult education, I examined the records of the 196 students actively enrolled during the fall semester of 1982 in the graduate program of the Department of Adult and Community Education at North Carolina State University. Of those 196, 96 were pursuing master's degrees and 100 were pursuing doctoral degrees. Distributions were calculated by broad categories. When those studying for the master's degree were compared to those pursuing doctoral degrees, the distribution of preparation at the bachelor's level was very similar. For those pursuing the doctoral degree, master's-level work had been in a field closely related to the bachelor-level work in most cases. Adult education had been pursued at the master's level in relatively few cases.

I classified prior academic preparation into (1) professional studies (including education), (2) behavioral/social sciences, (3) liberal arts, and (4) natural sciences. Professional studies dominated, accounting for 57 percent (112 of 196) of the cases. Nearly 44 percent (49 of 112) of those having pursued professional studies had studied in some area of education (largely secondary education). There was a wide variety of subject orientations in the study of secondary education, with home economics education being the single most frequent area, accounting for 20 percent of the 49 students who had studied education.

Home economics (not home economics education) represented the largest group in the professional studies category other than education (20 of 112). Nursing was next most frequent (13 of 112). Other majors were scattered widely. Those who had pursued studies in the behavioral sciences constituted the second largest group (24.5 percent; 48 of 196). Sociology/anthropology and history accounted for half the cases. Liberal arts studies accounted for 10.7 percent of the cases (21 of 196), with English being the dominant subject pursued. Natural sciences accounted for 7.7 percent (15 of 196), principally agricultural sciences.

These data may be relevant to the present topic in several ways. First, data from North Carolina State University may not be representative of all graduate programs. Second, in this instance, many of those who pursue the study of adult education have departed from earlier academic preparation; relatively few of the previous programs of study focused on adults as learners. The possible exceptions would be in home economics education and agricultural education, where, typically, some attention is given to adults as learners. Such shifts from earlier academic preparation are greater than for many other areas of graduate study.

Perhaps even more important is that students entering the study of adult education have experienced much of their academic study as passive receivers of information, rather than as seekers after potentially telling questions. They have studied in discipline-oriented environments, but they must function in problem-oriented environments. Most university teachers profess on their subjects, rather than helping students improve professional practice.

Most adult education graduate students have had professional experience. Many have also had some experience working with adults as learners. The professional study some have pursued previously has not enabled them to develop very adequate conceptual maps to guide their professional practice.

The Situation in Adult Education. An adequate perspective on preparing practitioners includes attention to the situations in which education of adults occurs. Most practitioners work with adult learners in nonformal settings, in which adults engage themselves freely to achieve their own purposes. In such settings, the adequacy of the activity is judged primarily by the learner.

Another factor to be considered in characterizing adult education is that the circumstances that lead adults to seek learning are diverse. These varying circumstances deserve to be considered in contemplating what is essential in the preparation of practicing adult educators. Four general types of situations are recognizable:

1. Adults sometimes seek assistance on a one-to-one basis for their

own individual purposes. An example would be a young mother who seeks help to know how to provide more adequate nutrition for a growing baby (by consulting a nutrition specialist or by taking a home study course).

2. Adults sometimes participate in a group learning activity, where each adult participates in pursuit of individual purposes. An example would be a temporary group of business people who seek to learn something related to accounting methods that might enable them to improve the efficiency of their individual record-keeping systems.

3. A group of adults with a collective purpose sometimes seeks assistance in learning something (for example, a community may seek help in resolving a problem with waste disposal). The problem cannot be dealt with by individuals pursuing their independent purposes. The people of the community seek help to learn how to deal collectively with a common problem that affects various segments of the community.

4. Institutions sometimes seek help to improve some of their functions. An institution may seek the assistance of an adult educator who, if a specialist, is often referred to an an organization-development specialist. The objectives and procedures in these settings are sufficiently different to warrant separate consideration. In such settings, what is required is what Argyris and Schön (1978) call organizational learning. An example would be a unit of county government, such as the social services department, seeking help to improve its ability to serve the needs of those citizens it was created to serve.

Except for the situation of individuals seeking help on a one-to-one basis, these four types of situations are conceptually different from the classification of clients as individuals, groups, and communities (Boyd and Apps, 1980). Each type of situation requires some competencies of the adult educator that are not required in the others. Many adult educators are called upon to deal with all four types of situations.

Universities offering graduate programs are strongly oriented toward courses of study aimed at extending knowledge. The strengthening of professional practice typically receives less emphasis. The ability to extend knowledge is prized and rewarded. In order to prepare practitioners more adequately, the university must make some substantial adjustments. First, students who major in adult education typically have not completed undergraduate study recently; their average age is about thirty-five. The majority have had extensive professional experience. Also, they have substantial personal obligations that make it difficult for them to devote extended periods of time to study. Thus, graduate programs should be highly efficient in time requirements and should focus on essentials.

Functioning in Professional Practice

Much of what a practitioner needs to know in order to function must be learned through personal inquiry. Some things the adult educator can be helped to learn have to do with modes of inquiry and bases for knowing what can introduce useful inquiry into specific situations.

A common fallacy in our professional literature is that adults know what they need to learn. For example, one credo identified by House (1972, p. 7) is that, because adults know what they need to learn, all that is required is to ask what they want to learn and then provide it. If this were true, the practitioner would be reactive, responding to requests from potential participants. Reflection on our own experience would demonstrate that, in fact, we frequently do not know specifically what we need to learn. Consequently, adult educators need to be proactive rather than just reactive. Being proactive includes both clarifying what needs to be learned and providing activities that will make it possible for the needed learning to occur.

Becoming Astute Students of the Work Environment. Effective practitioners are astute students of their work environments. Being students means they never know all they need to know; they are constantly seeking additional insights. Being astute means they are able to decide what to give attention to as they attempt to learn from their work environments. Thus, they should make their work situations laboratories for learning, as well as settings in which they must provide useful assistance to those with whom they work.

To help students become more astute in dealing with their work environments, graduate programs should enable them to learn to make connections between what is known and what is required of them in practice. We need to help them develop ways of thinking that will enable them to formulate strategies for doing. This requires bridging theory with practice. The practitioner functions as a user of knowledge for the purpose of dealing with and/or enabling others to deal with problems that arise in the normal conduct of human affairs. The practitioner role is problem-oriented, rather than discipline-oriented. Universities generate, examine, store, and disseminate knowledge. The practitioner can use that knowledge to formulate ways to deal with problems of practice.

Academic Preparation of Practitioners. Pursuing graduate study with a specialization in adult education should prepare students to engage in professional practice. Such graduate programs draw on various other subjects available in the university. This situation poses difficulty. When students of adult education take sociology courses, they are taught as if they were becoming sociologists. The same experience occurs in graduate courses in anthropology, statistics, economics, history, and psychology. But adult education graduate students are not studying to become sociologists or psychologists; they want to use ideas and processes dealt with in these subjects. Of all the concepts that could be learned from relevant scholarly disciplines, on what basis can concepts be selected that will be useful to practitioners?

The basis I propose for developing more adequate programs of study entails the identification of perspectives that enable professors to attend both to knowledge, as it is organized and available in the university, and, simultaneously, to the job to be done by the adult educator. These perspectives are at a level of generality that enables professors to develop programs of study that can be tailored to a wide range of particular interests and requirements. The intent is to help graduate students become increasingly astute students of their work environments.

Such perspectives should be useful both to professors and to students. Astute students of the work environment are not formed only from apprenticeships, nor does astuteness result only from a facility for professing on certain subjects. Instead, the desired perspectives depend on modes of thinking that enable practitioners to use organized knowledge to enhance practice. Generalizable processes and principles are needed.

The proposed perspectives are in response to the following question: What would adult educators need to consider in order to formulate adequate modes for responding to the problematic situations they encounter? Five perspectives represent my understanding of the range of matters involved in adult education practice. In earlier work (Carter, 1974) what are referred to here as *perspectives* were referred to as *areas of competence*.

Coping with the Work Environment. Adult educators should consider the many aspects of the milieu in which they function, because it constitutes an essential element with which they must cope. For example, the technologies of agriculture become a critical component of the work environment of agricultural extension educators or agents. There are social systems that impinge directly upon what practitioners are able to accomplish. Recognizing the social systems, considering their impact on the situation, and being able to use them as enabling mechanisms to accomplish an agency's mission are all assets. Ignoring those social systems can be a liability. Other important aspects of work environments include economic and political systems.

Systematic Inquiry. Being an astute student includes conducting inquiries. Much of the information practitioners need must be acquired through their own inquiries. We must learn how to engage in systematic inquiry. Curiosity is natural, but directing our curiosity into productive avenues requires systematic procedures. We become systematic by understanding not only ideas that enable us to formulate potentially telling questions but also the processes by which those questions can be pursued.

Coming to know what others have concluded as a result of their inquiries does not prepare us to inquire. For example, adult basic education practitioners must come to understand the goals and aspirations of nonliterates, their previous experience and existing understandings, their potential, their available resources, their proneness to risk taking, and so forth. Adult educators must gain insights into such factors through their own inquiries with the particular individuals with whom they are working.

Programming. Effective adult educators operate by well-formulated strategies. Their plans must be by their own design. They must plan in order to react adequately to problematic situations brought to their attention. Knowledge of effective program development strategies can enhance their practice. Doing something beyond reacting requires becoming proactive — engaging in systematic programming, designing plans and strategies to facilitate learning, and executing those strategies so that those being served are enabled to learn to deal with their own situations and aspirations more adequately. There are things the aspiring adult educator can learn that will contribute to such facility.

Human Behavior. There is substantial evidence that adult education practitioners are not intuitively able to understand the human factors involved in the forms of change we undertake to achieve and manage. Practitioners need an understanding of human communications at a relatively sophisticated level. Insights into human development and behavior are basic to understanding communications. Adult educators can acquire these insights by study.

Focusing on the Professional. The four perspectives introduced so far focus on areas of knowledge apart from the practitioner. Yet, as professionals, we are a vital component of the processes by which we accomplish our missions. Consequently, this fifth perspective focuses on the professional. This fifth perspective focuses on how practitioners come to think of themselves in the dynamics of their roles. The transition from being students to becoming practitioners involves increasing attention to organizational behavior. Practicing adult educators no longer pursue their own individual purposes and interests.

There is a body of knowledge about organizations, their management, how professionals relate to provider organizations and their components, how professionals relate to those they serve, how professionals organize themselves and interact in achieving shared purposes, and the like. This knowledge needs to become internalized as part of professional role perception.

These five perspectives are proposed as ways of thinking not only about what should go on as adult educators respond to problematic situations encountered in their work but also about what practitioners must be prepared to do in formulating useful ways of responding to those situations. Educational preparation should help practitioners consider all five perspectives in their professional practice.

Some preliminary inquiry has been undertaken regarding whether these five perspectives can be used in thinking about problematic situations actually encountered by extension workers. McLoughlin (1972) worked with a sample of critical-incident accounts he collected from extension workers in Ireland. He examined each critical incident from each of the five perspectives. Each perspective helped him extend his analysis. He raised different questions with each of the five perspectives, concluding that the combination of questions raised with the five perspectives represented the range of critical questions that would need to be considered.

Most Pressing Needs

An adequate curriculum for preparing adult educators must focus on substance rather than just on form. Form is illustrated by numbers of credits, courses to be taken, and other requirements to be met. A focus on substance includes attention to what is to occur in the experiences of students as they engage in courses. Adequate substance for a graduate curriculum in adult education should provide for three broad categories of experience for students, plus a fourth area that cuts across these three:

1. Students should study critically and analytically the thoughts, experiences, inquiries, and scholarly speculations of others — in other words, what is contained in the professional and scholarly literature and what arises out of direct contact with faculty members. The essential feature is critical and analytical study of the literature and of what is presented orally by faculty members and others.

2. Students should also directly experience aspects of the practice of adult education. Activities such as internships and field experiences can be provided. The learner needs concrete examples about which to think — examples that can provide meaning to the abstractions acquired from the literature.

3. Students need exercises in reflecting. Such reflecting involves enabling adult education students to (1) get in touch with their own previous experiences, (2) make conceptual and operational sense out of those activities observed directly during the course of study, and (3) contemplate possible consequences of using the concepts and processes being considered.

4. This category of experience cuts across the three broad categories already listed and is typically absent from academic programs. Students preparing to become practitioners need to have learning activities that provide opportunities for rehearsing the use of conceptual ideas and processes in nonthreatening environments in which equally nonthreatening feedback can be received. The environments for rehearsing should be as similar as possible to those encountered in practice. Argyris (1982, pp. 451–467) discusses this category of experience in the context of creating conditions for "double-loop learning" in social systems.

For students to become increasingly astute at engaging in these four proposed categories of experience and develop growing competence to function as practitioners, two of the five perspectives (areas of competence) are most critical, in my judgment. The first is the facility for engaging in systematic inquiry. Graduate students typically are required to engage in the most formalized mode of systematic inquiry, research. Important as facility in research may be, it may be more important to engage in a whole range of modes of systematic inquiry, from the least formalized (what we take in and consider in the course of our other daily professional activities) to the most formalized. The less formalized modes seem to receive little attention. The second most critical perspective concerns facilitating learning in others. Most graduate programs with which I am familiar are noticeably deficient in this regard. Most programs provide substantial planning activity at a broad general level, but conscious effort to develop adequate conceptual and operational bases for facilitating learning is unusual. Yet, the basic premise for the role of educator has to do with enabling others to learn. That premise applies whether the aspiring practitioner is concerned with increasing competence as an administrator, a planner, or a programmer. Developing a perspective on and a facility for enabling others to learn is part of the more general perspective (area of competence) outlined earlier and referred to as *programming.*

It will not be easy to provide opportunities for graduate students to develop these two most critical perspectives. We have had too much experience as receivers of information to shift easily to an orientation of developing (1) adequate cognitive maps and processes for engaging in purposeful inquiry and (2) a stance that doing so is not only appropriate but also imperative. It will be equally difficult to make the needed shift toward a more adequate orientation to facilitating learning. Most of us, as a result of years of experience, have come to believe that teaching is telling—that when learners have had an opportunity to hear, they have been provided ample opportunity to learn.

Summary

Graduate education is increasing its commitment to enabling those who participate to become more adequate adult educators. The arena in which this effort occurs presents some challenges. Among those challenges are (1) the orientations that prompt participants' pursuit of graduate study, (2) their prior academic preparation and experience, and (3) the nature of the environments in which adult education occurs. Equally challenging to those who attempt to design and provide adequate academic preparation for practitioner adult educators is the nature of the institutions in which that academic preparation can occur. Universities that sanction and reward the development, testing, and extension of knowledge have difficulty in recognizing the legitimacy of programs aimed primarily at applying knowledge to practice.

Aspiring adult education practitioners must draw on a range of knowledge and processes. These practitioners must be designers and implementers of learning opportunities that enable their learners to cope more adequately with their own living and working situations and aspirations. Developing the capacity and competence to function in such a milieu requires having access to a curriculum that draws on accumulated knowledge and enables participants to incorporate this knowledge into the very nature of the functions required of practitioners.

A constellation of five perspectives is postulated to provide a basis for (1) acquiring and selecting knowledge that has been accumulated, organized, and stored, (2) providing a conceptual map for connecting essential knowledge to professional functions, and (3) organizing those areas of competence required of practitioners.

It is not contended that accomplishing what is being proposed, as needed, will be easy. To the contrary, there are strongly engrained accumulations of experience militating against the perspective being proposed here. Overcoming the obstacles will involve focusing attention on the substance (the dynamics) of the graduate curriculum, rather than on its form. Four categories of experience have been proposed as the basis for such substance.

Finally, the two perspectives (areas of competence) most inadequately provided for in present curricula have been identified as (1) systematic inquiry and (2) facilitating learning (a component of programming). Improving upon existing conditions will require bold and imaginative activity on the part of faculties responsible for the graduate preparation of adult educators.

References

Argyris, C. *Reasoning, Learning, and Action: Individual and Organizational.* San Francisco: Jossey-Bass, 1982.

Argyris, C., and Schön, D. A. *Organizational Learning: A Theory of Action Perspective.* Reading, Mass.: Addison-Wesley, 1978.

Boyd, R. D., and Apps, J. W., and Associates. *Redefining the Discipline of Adult Education.* San Francisco: Jossey-Bass, 1980.

Carter, G. L., Jr. "Developing and Testing a New Conceptual Formulation for Determining Curricula for the Practitioner: A Case." Paper presented at the Adult Education Research Conference, Chicago, April 18, 1974.

Clark, A. *Adult Development and the Experience of Graduate Education: A Review of the Literature.* San Francisco: Association for Humanistic Psychology, 1980.

Houle, C. O. *The Design of Education.* San Francisco: Jossey-Bass, 1972.

McLoughlin, M. "A Critical-Incident Study of Agricultural Inspectors in the Department of Agriculture and Fisheries." Unpublished master's thesis, National University of Ireland, 1972.

G. L. Carter has been a professor in the Department of Adult and Community College Education at North Carolina State University since 1980. Prior to 1980, he worked in the Department of Continuing and Vocational Education at the University of Wisconsin–Madison and the University of Wisconsin–Extension. The ideas developed in this chapter evolved from experiences in the United States, Western Europe, Southeast Asia, and South America.

Index

A

Accreditation: of Dale Carnegie courses, 25; of professional continuing education, 68; of trade schools, 22
Adult educators: academic preparation of, 77-78; analysis of preparation of, 73-82; as astute students of work environment, 77; characteristics of, as students, 74-75; and coping with work environment, 78; as facilitators of learning, 81; graduate study for, 74-76; human behavior understanding by, 79; most pressing needs in preparing, 80-81; and professional focus, 79; professional functioning of, 76-80; programming by, 79, 81; situations in practice of, 75-76; summary on, 81-82; systematic inquiry by, 78, 80-81
American Association of Medical Colleges, 68
American Institute for Research, 24
American Medical Association (AMA), 64, 70
Anderson, A., 66, 70
Apps, J. W., 76, 82
Archambault, L., 33, 36
Argyris, C., 76, 80, 82
Army Continuing Education System (ACES), 38-39
Army Training and Evaluation Program, 41
Attitudes: in Dale Carnegie courses, 26, 28; and management, 15-16

B

Bennett, C., 56
Berdie, D. R., 56
Better Business Bureau, 22
Black, R., 56
Bloom, B. S., 12, 19
Botticelli, M., 66, 70
Boyd, R. D., 76, 82
Bradburn, N., 56
Bridgman, M. S., 43
Brodsky, N., 37, 42

Brown, C. R., Jr., 59, 70
Bruce, R. L., 2, 45-57
Buckholtz, M., 35, 36
Byrn, D., 56

C

Carnegie, D., 25-26, 28
Carter, G. L., Jr., 3, 73-82
Chellino, S. N., 1, 11-19
Cheung, M., 64, 70
Chronic obstructive pulmonary disease (COPD), 61, 63, 64
Clark, A., 73, 82
Clute, K. F., 64, 70
Cohen, R., 64, 71
Community colleges: analysis of occupational programs in, 31-36; curriculum at, 34-35; faculty role at, 35; guidelines for occupational education in, 35-36; and student needs, 31-33
Continuing Education Council, 25
Continuing Education Systems Project, 68
Cooperative extension: analysis of evaluation in, 45-57; Extension Management Information System (EMIS) in, 54-55; local involvement with, 47-48; monitoring in, 54; organization of, 45-46; and participation in evaluation, 53-54; resources on, 56; single-use plans in, 46-47
Coordinating Council on Medical Education, 65, 70
Corbett, A. J., 12, 19
Corbett, J. J., 2, 31-36
Corcoran, P., 64, 68, 70
Cosby, A. G., 56
Cost effectiveness, need for, 12-13
Costello, G., 66, 70
Cotoia, A. M., 33, 36
Coué, É., 28
Council for Noncollegiate Continuing Education, 25
Coyne, J., 24, 29
Cross, H., 59, 70

83

D

Dale Carnegie courses: accreditation of, 25; analysis of, 25-29; attitudes in, 26, 28; educational philosophy of, 27-28; founder of, 25-26; influences on, 28-29; instructional techniques in, 28; pedagogical approach of, 26-27
Decisions: periodic, 48-49, 50; settings for, 48-51
Dewey, J., 26, 28
Dinneen, M., 12, 19
Drucker, P. F., 5, 10, 14, 19
Duff, W., 64, 70
Duncan, W. J., 32, 36

E

Education: for adult educators, 77-78; in community colleges, 31-36; through cooperative extension, 45-57; guidelines for increasing impact of, 3; by military services, 37-43; performance and accountability demanded in, 5; professional continuing, 59-72; in proprietary schools, 21-29; training distinct from, 6, 42
Escovitz, G., 59, 71
Evaluation: for accountability, 48, 49; CIPP model of, 48-51, 53; context, 49; in cooperative extension, 45-57; Countenance model of, 53; criteria for, 52-53; and decision setting, 48-51; guidelines for, 55; input, 49-50; for monitoring, 48-49, 51, 54; participation in, 53-54; as practical process, 48; process, 50; process of, 51-53; product, 50-51; resources on, 55-56
Extension Management Information System (EMIS), 54-55

F

Faculty: at community colleges, 35; at trade schools, 24
Fiedler, J., 56
Flair, M. D., 7, 9, 10
Fleisher, D., 60, 71
Fontelle, G., 36
Fort Dix, 39
Fox, L. C., 42
Fromm, E., 28

G

Gagné, R., 27, 29
Gilbert, T. F., 11, 12, 19
Gonnella, J., 2, 59-72
Goodman, L. V., 34, 36
Goran, M., 66, 71
Gordon, J. J., 34, 36
Grabowski, S. M., 1-10
Grassi-Stimson, L., 6, 10
Griner, P., 65, 71
Gross, J., 56
Guba, E., 55

H

Haines, P. G., 35, 36
Harding, F. D., 39, 42
Harless, J. H., 11, 12, 13, 19
Harper, W., 33, 36
Harzberg, F., 16, 19
Hassanein, R., 64, 71
Hauke, R. N., 42
Herbert, T., 24, 29
Houle, C. O., 6, 10, 29, 77, 82

J

James, W., 28
Job market, competencies demanded in, 6
Joint Commission on the Accreditation of Hospitals, 64, 71

K

Kidd, J. R., 29
King, D. C., 18, 19
Knowles, M. S., 26, 28, 29

L

Land-grant universities, and cooperative extension, 46, 47-48
Larson, G., 2, 37-43
Latham, G. P., 18, 19
Learning: facilitation of, 81; transfer of, 7, 9, 27
Lessinger, L., 63, 71
Levine, H., 66, 71
Lewis, A., 63, 71
Lewis, C., 64, 71
Lincoln, Y. S., 55
Lusterman, S., 6, 10

M

McAuliff, W., 65, 71
McCabe, M., 35, 36
McCarthy, W., 66, 71
McGoff, R. M., 39, 42
McGuire, C., 66, 71
Mackey, P. J., 1-2, 21-29
McLoughlin, M., 79-80, 82
Maeroff, G. I., 21, 29
Mager, R. F., 11, 19, 34, 36

Maier, N. R. F., 14, 15, 19
Management: analysis of training merged with, 11-19; and attitude, 15-16; discussion and conclusions regarding, 17-19; performance improvement in, 14-16; problem in, 13-14; and punishment, 15; solutions in, 14-17; and work standards, 15
Marland, S. P., 33, 36
Maslow, A. H., 28
Mason, P. E., 35, 36
Mausner, B., 16, 19
May, R., 28
Military: adult education by, 37; analysis of education and training in, 37-43; Army training system in, 39-41; basic skills education in, 39; and Code of Conduct, 40; evaluation and feedback in, 41-42; role of education in, 38-39; role of training in, 38
Miller, G. E., 59, 71
Miller, R. W., 56
Missouri State Teachers College (Central Missouri State University), 25
Monitoring: and evaluation, 48-49, 51, 54; of training, 17
Mosel, J. N., 6, 9, 10
Myers, L. B., 43

N

National Association of Trade and Technical Schools (NATTS), 21, 22, 23n, 24, 25, 29
National Center for Education Statistics, 29
North Carolina State University, Department of Adult and Community Education at, 74-75

O

Occupational education: in community colleges, 31-36; guidelines for, 35-36; purposes of, 32-33. *See also* Trade schools
Odiorne, G. S., 14, 19
Oliver, A. I., 35, 36
Osborne, C., 60, 71

P

Payne, B., 66, 71
Payne, S. L., 56
Performance: criteria for ideal, 60-62; diagnosis of deficiencies in, 63-65; ensuring, 5-10; evaluation as guarantee of, 45-57; future-oriented, 9; guidelines for improving, 18-19; improvement strategy for, 14-16; influences on, 60; on-the-job follow-through for, 7-8; and professional education, 59-72; proficiency related to, 61, 63, 65-66; and situational factors, 63-64
Personalized System of Instruction (PSI), for occupational education, 32, 35
Peterson, O., 64, 71
Pifer, A., 32, 36
Pipe, P., 11, 19
Popham, W. J., 55
Problems: causes of, 12; defined, 11
Professional continuing education: accreditation for, 68; analysis of, 59-72; cost-benefit studies of, 69-70; diagnostic checklist for, 67; goal of, 61; performance orientation of, 68-70; program structure and learners' needs in, 66-67; and quality control, 69
Professional-standards review organizations (PSROs), 69
Proficiency: evaluation of impact of, 65-66; performance related to, 61, 63, 65-66
Proprietary schools: analysis of, 21-29; and Dale Carnegie courses, 25-29; functions of, 21; vocational education at, 21-25
Pueblo incident, and military training, 40
Puerta, I., 56

R

Renberg, T., 35, 36
Research Triangle Institute, Center for Educational Research and Evaluation of, 31-32
Rice, R. L., 12, 19
Richards, R., 64, 71
Rogers, C., 28
Rossi, P. H., 55
Rossinger, G., 43

S

Schön, D. A., 76, 82
Skinner, B. F., 27
Smith, M. E., 12, 19
Snyderman, B. B., 16, 19
Solmon, L. C., 34, 35
Solutions: criteria for, 12; in management, 14-17
Spitzer, D. R., 7, 10
Stake, R., 53, 56
Starry, D. A., 38, 42

Steele, S. M., 56
Sticht, T. G., 39, 42
Stock, J. R., 43
Storey, P., 63, 65, 71
Stritter, F. T., 7, 9, 10
Stufflebeam, D., 48, 53, 56
Sudman, S., 56
Suter, E., 68, 71
Swanson, G. I., 32, 36

T

Thorndike, E. L., 27
Tolchinsky, P. D., 18, 19
Tough, A., 29
Trade schools: accreditation of, 22; analysis of, 21-25; certification of completion from, 22, 24; curriculum at, 24; dropouts from, 24; evaluation of, 24-25; faculty at, 24; skill training available at, 23. *See also* Occupational education
Training: education distinct from, 6, 42; implementation of, 16-17; management merged with, 11-19; monitoring of, 17; for performance improvement, 14-16

U

U.S. Army Training and Doctrine Command (TRADOC), 38, 39, 40, 42
U.S. Department of Agriculture, 46, 47, 56; Science and Education Administration of, 46
U.S. Department of Defense, 37
U.S. Department of Health, Education, and Welfare, 65, 69, 71
U.S. Department of the Army, 38, 39, 42-43

V

Vess, D. M., 32, 36
Veterans Administration, 68
Vocational education. *See* Occupational education; Trade schools

W

Walker, R. J., 1, 11-19
Warwick, D. P., 56
Weed, L., 59, 72
Welling, J. R., 38, 43
Wetherill, G. R., 56
Wexler, H., 32, 36
White, C. W., 60, 72
Whiteley, T., 34, 36
Williams, W., 55
Williamson, J., 66, 71

Y

Yankelovitch, D., 34, 36
Youel, D. B., 60, 64, 72
Yuki, G. A., 18, 19

Z

Zapf, D. W., 42
Zeleznik, C., 2, 59-72